ERROL FLYNN SLEPT HERE

ERROL FLYNN SLEPT HERE

The Flynns, the Hamblens, Ricky Nelson, and the Most Notorious House in Hollywood

Robert Matzen and Michael Mazzone

GoodKnight Books
Pittsburgh, Pennsylvania

GoodKnight Books

© 2009 by Paladin Communications

Published by GoodKnight Books, an imprint of Paladin Communications
Pittsburgh, Pennsylvania

Printed in the United States of America

First Edition

Library of Congress Control Number: 2008940021

ISBN 978-0-9711685-7-2

frontispiece: Errol Flynn's Mulholland Farm by Bert Six

(John McElwee Collection)

CONTENTS

hat a strange topic for a book…Errol Flynn's house. It wasn't the grandest home in the sprawling set of duchies that bear the collective designation of "Hollywood." It didn't have the biggest living space, to the surprise and sometimes disappointment of casual visitors who expected a castle. It wasn't the best designed, but rather has been described as a "mishmash." It often wasn't clean and green; the winds channeling through the gorges blew dirt into the windows and the pool and the tennis court. It wasn't easily accessible; the prospective visitor traveling in bad weather or at night risked life and limb. What Errol Flynn's house had going for it was Errol Flynn.

Writer Earl Conrad, who ghostwrote with Flynn the memoir *My Wicked, Wicked Ways,* tried to pinpoint the world's enduring fascination with Flynn:

"The remarkability of him was his individuality, his uniqueness, a certain independence and even wildness, as if he were an untamed brother of the sky, like the wild geese that fly overhead while domesticated geese in their barnyard warrens are limited to looking upward yearningly at the free-flying geese overhead, going hundreds of miles a day north or south."

We earthbound humans dream our dreams of adventure, lovemaking, sailing, flying, wealth, beauty, conquest. He lived all of them, every day.

Within the reminiscences of the people who knew him, the three words that appear most often are "larger than life," alluding to a genuine swashbuckler, a quintessential human being with all the blessings and all the flaws of creation wrapped up in a six-foot, two-inch collection of molecules. He entertained. He created. He inspired. He experimented. He destroyed. He made love. He hated. Part poet and part sadist, in one breath charming and in the next cruel, a fabulous-looking guy who could appear genuinely ugly—and he did all this in 50 short years.

This wasn't just any house. This was *his* house.

The story of the house on Mulholland Drive doesn't end with Errol Flynn. The place that he had made famous and infamous and notorious and perverted would endure for more than 30 years after he left it, and it would be owned by two men who were also described as "larger than life," giving this particular house quite the pedigree.

Stuart Hamblen's name today lacks the weight that it carried 50 years ago when he hobnobbed with John Wayne, Roy Rogers, and Ronald Reagan, and wrote hit songs, and broadcast a radio show that was number one on the West Coast and syndicated across the country. But Hamblen lived at Mulholland during 20 of his most productive and successful years, and to this day, the Hamblens view Mulholland as part of the family.

Ricky Nelson's name has endured more for his presence on a hit TV series that ran 14 seasons than for his first love, and his great talent, music. Nelson lived at Mulholland for six-plus years, along with his children, Tracy, twins Matthew and Gunnar, and youngest son Sam. And Rick Nelson would die owning Mulholland, loving the idea of it being Flynn's house. For Nelson, Mulholland was a place to hide his pain, in the quiet and the dark, for long stretches at a time.

This strange topic for a book begins in the South Seas and ends in Texas, but no matter how far its three fearless owners strayed, they remained anchored to one place that is burned into the memories of everyone who knew them and visited there. That place is Mulholland Farm.

– Robert Matzen, August 2008

All my life, I have wanted to write about Hollywood history. A house would seem an unlikely subject. After all, how much can you write about a house, even if it is a celebrity's home in Hollywood? To my knowledge, no one has ever devoted an entire book to a film star's home, although some worthy subjects come to mind—Doug and Mary's Pickfair and Harold Lloyd's Greenacres. For me, it is Errol Flynn's Mulholland Farm.

On a June day in 1987, I walked through Mulholland Farm. In the hour or so that I was there, Mulholland revealed few of its secrets to me. Little did I know of the hidden passageways, peepholes, two-way mirrors, and the resident ghost that virtually all of Mulholland's residents would come to know. For all that, I would have to wait.

Although my time there was brief, I took almost 100 35mm photos of the house and grounds.

Less than a year after my visit to Mulholland, author William Donati contacted me and inquired whether I had a photo of Errol's pal, Hollywood stuntman Buster Wiles, at Mulholland Farm. Unfortunately, I did not, and Bill, who

was working on his excellent book, *My Days with Errol Flynn* (1988), told me that he and Buster had recently spent an afternoon at Mulholland and that the house had been gutted to the point that only bare studs with dangling wiring remained where there had once been walls. I was shocked. When I got off the phone with Bill, I revisited my photos, now knowing that what once had been, was no more.

When I photographed the house in 1987, little had changed since the Flynn days. Now, the house had been permanently altered, and I realized I may have the last record of its unaltered state. Soon after, I was contacted by a friend and fellow Flynn fan, Trudy McVicker, who asked for a couple sets of my Mulholland pictures. She also wondered if it would be too much trouble for me to provide captions as a kind of virtual tour.

More than a year had passed since I took the photos, and I was unsure about what went where. Eventually I had to refer to my negative strips to verify the order in which I had taken the photos. I sketched a floor plan of the house to indicate the areas where I had taken each photo. I tried to read as much as I could find about the house. I sent the photos to Trudy, and she put them in a binder and added my captions to make a booklet. To Trudy, I am grateful for making me realize that in some small way, I had helped to record part of Hollywood history.

In the fall of 1988, filmmaker and lifelong Flynn fan Jack Marino called to tell me that Mulholland House had been torn down. Shortly thereafter, Jack sent me a photo of the ruins with a lone chimney standing—the very fireplace that I had proudly posed in front of less than a year and a half earlier and where Errol had posed for Warner Brothers photographer Bert Six some 45 years before that. Errol Flynn's Mulholland House had become a teardown—a house that is purchased not for the home, but for the property upon which it sits. When it comes to real estate in Hollywood, nothing is sacred.

– Michael Mazzone, August 2008

Acknowledgments

This isn't a book that just happened. It was inspired by events the authors experienced at Mulholland Farm in 1987. Years before that, Robert Matzen knew and worked with people who had been important to the life of Errol Flynn, including Nora Eddington Black, Earl Conrad, Patric Knowles, Robert Stack, and Tony Thomas. Information shared with these notables in previous projects has proved invaluable to the creation of this book.

Our thanks to the following people for helping to make *Errol Flynn Slept Here* a reality: Rudy and Stacey Behlmer, Tulley Hamblen Brown, Frank Bruno, Leda Carmody, J. Robert Cullen, James DeMarco, Robert Florczak, Deirdre Flynn, Suzy Hamblen, Michael Hawks, Steven Hayes, Laurie Jacobson, Mike Johnson, Kim Jaserie, Lisa Obee Hamblen-Jaserie, Sandra Joy Lee & the Warner Brothers Archive at USC, Joan Leslie, Bill Lindsay, Bob Lindsay, the staff of the Margaret Herrick Library, Jack Marino, Louise Marino, Terri Mazzone, John McElwee, Regan McMahon, John Hammond Moore, Liz Motley, Gunnar Nelson, Matthew Nelson, Mike Pappas, Gary Payne, Harve Presnell, Cheryl Rogers-Barnett, Gary Vaughn, Marc Wanamaker, and Judy Whisenant.

Thanks also go to the outstanding team that produced this book, including editor and project manager Mary Matzen, designers Sharon Berk and Lisa Weyandt, production manager Julie Tabaka, and graphic artist Valerie Sloan.

Some wild charges have been leveled at Errol Flynn over the years. None have ever been proven; most or all have been debunked. The authors would like to acknowledge that they will not give credibility to the unsubstantiated conclusions drawn by previous authors by repeating them in *Errol Flynn Slept Here*. Instead, we have focused our work on credible sources that can be substantiated and eyewitness accounts wherever possible.

Above: Author Robert Matzen sits on the Mulholland Farm diving board. (Photo by Gary Vaughn) Below: Author Mike Mazzone strikes a Flynn pose in the den. Page 90 shows a vintage shot of this location. (Photo by Terri Mazzone)

Introduction

March 1987

If the fence had been locked properly, I wouldn't have shinnied through, and there would be no *Errol Flynn Slept Here*. It was March 19, 1987, while my (then) wife Debra and I were in Hollywood from Pittsburgh to conduct research for a book about Carole Lombard. We had taken a day for sightseeing with Gary Vaughn, a friend and film history buff, and found ourselves winding our way up Mulholland Drive on a sunny, dry, and very warm day.

Mulholland is a long roadway that snakes along the crest of the San Fernando Mountains. It bisects some of the richest acreage in the world, where movie stars build their homes because of its status as high-value real estate and its relative seclusion from film studios, fans, and the hubbub of the motion picture business.

Right on schedule, according to the tour book guiding us, Flynn's house popped into view as a gleaming stretch of white set into the sagebrush hillside. We followed the instructions in the book and turned off of Mulholland.

At the end of a side street stood two brick posts painted white and a pair of iron gates. Beyond, in the dry, hot silence sat a decaying frame house. This dingy, ordinary place had been Party Central to the stars and the most notorious home in Hollywood?

We climbed out of our rental car and stood in the midday heat. Most shocking was the For Sale sign. The house sat empty, padlocked, and alone. Except for us. We gawked

for a while and paid our respects to the house. Gary said, in his Tennessee drawl, "We aren't gonna go ee-in?" Well, no. We could be arrested for trespassing, I said, and Debra agreed. But a plan evolved in seconds anyway because of the once-in-a-lifetime nature of the opportunity. We were going to spend a few moments seeing what Errol Flynn's world looked like.

I squeezed my way through the slack-jawed gate easily, and Gary followed. From *My Wicked, Wicked Ways*, Flynn's autobiography, I knew of this house, its history, and its importance to Flynn. It had been his creation, his dream, his glory, and his refuge.

We walked around the garage and the west wing, where I could smell dry-rotting wood. I knew then that the place was doomed. Suddenly we could see it all, the front of the house, the lawn, the pool. The place known as Errol Flynn's Mulholland Farm was a rambling, two-story colonial with dormers.

We wandered over to the pool; Gary took my photo on the diving board. We drifted along the house, snapping photos. It looked like any other empty house inside—lots of bare white walls and half-opened doors.

Gary posed near the back door, and I snapped another photo. There was a wine cellar tucked into the foundation, its door yawning open. I descended the steps hoping to find a passage that went up and into the house, but there was none. Just empty wooden wine racks and the guts of an old radio.

We had paid our respects to Errol Flynn and Hollywood history, and we departed.

The next day, when I should have been working on the Lombard book, the visit to Mulholland was still on my mind, and Debra and I went back, this time without my camera, with nothing but my eyes and my memory, and I wandered around and drank the place in, in the dead quiet and the dry March heat. I stood with the pool between me and the house and just looked at this fine old piece of Hollywood history.

As I paid my homage, I became aware that I wasn't alone. It hit me all at once: someone was watching me from a second-floor window. It's one of those moments when the hairs go up on your neck. I remarked to myself: Errol Flynn's house is haunted. And then, just as quickly: Nah, you're imagining things.

Back home in Pennsylvania, I called my friend, Mike Mazzone, an avid film buff. I told him about the two visits to the Farm, and that the place was for sale, and that Debra had inquired about it and been told the asking price was $1.1 million. Mike and his bride were already scheduled to go to Hollywood in three months, and so he planned to make his own visit to Mulholland Farm, hoping to have an experience similar to mine. He did, and then again he didn't. But that is his story to tell.

Robert Matzen

June 1987

On a cold day in Southern Ohio in March 1987, my phone rang, and Bob told me of his adventures at Errol Flynn's house. Wow! What a story! He also informed me that he had called the real estate agent and learned that the price was set at $1.1 million. I was planning a trip to L.A. in June. What if I contacted the real estate office as a prospective buyer and arranged a tour?

Not long before our departure date, Bob called again to tell me that the house had been sold. So much for my plan to tour Mulholland. In mid-June, my wife, Terri, and I flew to California. On June 19, we drove to the Fynn house. It sat off a quiet street, Torreyson Place, which dead ends into the hillside at a circle drive, once Errol's driveway. No one was around, and the gates were open. I looked up the driveway and could see the gables of the house. I asked Terri if she wanted to walk up with me. She said, "You go on up. I'm OK." Terri was three months pregnant at the time, so I left her sitting in the car reading a book.

Walking up the drive, I saw an old truck and a dumpster near the garage. I will never forget how dead quiet it was. I walked around the house, and I heard muffled voices. Further along, near the pool sat a cluster of Mexican gardeners, eating lunch and talking. I strolled up to them.

"Excuse me," I said, "but I just got in from Ohio and, well, this used to be Errol Flynn's house. Would you care if I walked around and took some pictures?" A half dozen guys stared back at me. The one who seemed to be in charge reminded me of the man in the gold hat from *The Treasure of the Sierra Madre*.

"Si, Ohio," he said, "that is a long way." I figured he didn't have the slightest idea how far and didn't really care.

I told him I had always wanted to see Errol Flynn's house. "Si! Errrol Fleeeen, beeeg star!" Then he said, "Sure, go on eeeen, the door is open."

Go on in? The door is open? I couldn't believe it. He sat there by the diving board, smiling at me. I walked to the door, pushed it open, and gaped inside. The house was empty, and there wasn't a soul around. I hurried around the west wing. Once out of sight, I sprinted down the driveway. There was Terri sitting in the car with her nose buried in her book. "Come on!" I said. "The place is wide open. There are Mexican gardeners up there, and they said we can go inside!"

"Are you nuts?" said my wife. "You don't know those people." Nope, and I didn't care. They said I could go inside Errol Flynn's house and that was good enough for me. I grabbed my camera bag and up the driveway we went. I started taking photos as we walked. I shot everything that looked important: the gates, the exterior of the house, the wine cellar—everything. There was a set of wooden stairs that looked ready to fall apart. We kept walking and found the gardeners still eating their lunch.

The living room without furniture was huge. Right off, I saw the formal fireplace. "That's the fireplace where the Decker painting used to hang," I told Terri. I remembered the famous photo of Errol posing next to the painting. I insisted that Terri recreate the moment with me posed in the same spot, and then we hurried on.

I photographed each wall, each room, even the bathrooms. I had a regular 50mm lens and a 28mm wide angle lens that got more width in closed areas. Sometimes I used a flash, and sometimes I relied on the natural light. I shot off a roll and reloaded. We went into the den. There was another fireplace. Afraid that I had posed in front of the wrong one, I had Terri take another shot. Then we went into an even larger room in the east wing, and it had a fireplace, and I made Terri take yet another picture.

Set off from the great room in the east wing was a bedroom. I walked in and noticed that it had a mirrored ceiling made up of glass panels. Could this be the two-way mirror? I knew that a trick mirror doesn't have silvering on the back side. Sure enough, one of the panels had an unusual cast to it. This was where Flynn would look down at couples making love. Almost 50 years later, the infamous two-way mirror still existed.

I took more photos, and Terri warned, "You better slow down." But I wasn't listening. We covered the whole downstairs—dining room, kitchen, garage. By the dining room stood a spiral staircase, and up we went. I made a turn into one of the guest bedrooms. It had a small porch that overlooked the garage. Years later I read that one of Rick Nelson's sons said he'd be awakened by his father starting his Pantera late at night as he went for a drive on Mulholland. I am sure this must have been the son's bedroom, as the garage was directly below. We went into another bedroom. Down the hall heading toward the master bedroom was a series of clothes closets. I took a shot in the hall, and I had come to the end of a roll of film. I reached in my camera bag for another roll. I was out of film.

Terri reminded me, "I told you you were taking too many pictures."

I said, "We'll have to go get more film and come back."

Terri thought we had pressed our luck enough. She said, "Where are you going to go to get film around here?"

It was mighty desolate indeed. But what other choice was there?

I asked the foreman if we could leave and come right back. He said that was fine. Off we went on Mulholland toward Laurel Canyon. Mulholland is a winding road with hairpin turns that overlooks sheer cliffs. I was driving way too fast, and the suspension in the mid-80s Grand Prix was pretty soft. And Terri was prone to morning sickness. She warned me to slow down *or else.*

I flew over Laurel Canyon toward the Valley. At Laurel and Ventura I spotted a pharmacy, bought my film, hung a U on Ventura, careened back onto Laurel, and floored it for Mulholland. I bet Rick Nelson couldn't have made the trip any faster in his Pantera than I did that day. In minutes we were at the house, reloaded and shooting.

Into Errol Flynn's large and formal-looking bedroom we went. There was another fireplace; I had Terri take my picture (just in case). Out the window I could see the workmen clearing brush on the hillside. Here I was, standing in the most private room at Errol's beloved Mulholland Farm. From another window I could see the pool below.

We made our way back downstairs and outside, where I took some pictures around the pool. I walked over to a brick-and-flagstone stairway beyond a set of gates. Stone lions stood guard. The steps led to the tennis court below. When we had seen it all, we reluctantly walked down the driveway.

I still couldn't believe what I had just experienced. It was as if Errol had invited me up for the day, but he never showed up, perhaps detained by an alluring blonde. I looked over my shoulder at the place one last time, and we got in the car and drove away. If I had been there a day earlier or a day later, I would not have been afforded the same opportunity. So it was that fate smiled on me one day 20 years ago, helping to make this book possible.

Michael Mazzone

ERROL FLYNN SLEPT HERE

Errol Flynn, age 25, steps off the boat at the port of New York, bad teeth and all, and poses for a Warner Brothers photographer. Ever optimistic, Flynn states on his immigration form that he hopes to spend six months in the picture business. (John McElwee Collection)

Errol Flynn will live a life not unlike that of a man he will portray on-screen, George Armstrong Custer. Custer had been an ambitious man of boyish charm, ambiguous morals, and considerable abilities, who became world famous and grew to believe in his own luck. Custer's Luck. He was also utterly fearless in all situations. And when he began to rely on Custer's Luck, he got himself butchered in Montana.

Flynn is, for a decade and a half, as adored for his looks as Brad Pitt; as prototypical a ladies man as Christian Bale; as charming and laid back as George Clooney. Flynn ranks as the most popular action hero in motion pictures, all six-foot-two of him expressed in lean muscle and physical movement so graceful that he appears to defy gravity with every step. He lives a carefree, adventurous life. He is also fearless in the face of physical or moral danger. And when he starts to rely on his luck, he will get himself butchered in his own version of Custer's Last Stand.

Flynn's early life is well documented; he is born in Tasmania on June 20, 1909, to Theodore Thomson Flynn and Lily Mary Young. Late in his life Flynn will send a letter to his ghostwriter, Earl Conrad, with changes to his soon-to-be-released autobiography. In this letter Flynn describes a scandal he has recently uncovered. Looking at his own birth certificate, he relates to Conrad that his parents were married on January 23, 1909, and he was born a mere five months later. "Oh, Mother! Really, how could you!" says Flynn in mock horror.[1] Flynn recommends to Conrad that this information and this quote open the book, and he writes the scenario in full in the letter. Whether

because of libel issues or because of approaching deadlines, this information will not make the final cut of *My Wicked, Wicked Ways,* but the episode does much to illuminate the lifelong conflict between mother and son that shapes his character and leads him into a great deal of mischief.

Conrad says later of Flynn, "She instilled in him the thought that sex, the genitals, were sinful. He received from that baptism a fear and a confusion, plus an abnormal concern about sex."[2]

Lily's messages are mixed from the beginning. Young Errol sees the attention that men pay his attractive mother; he sees her flirtatious manner in return. Yet she tells him that sex equals sin.

Would the 21-year-old Lily have married biology professor Theo if she hadn't been forced into it by pregnancy? If the answer is no, who is there for her to blame if not the child who had become the trap? Lily's extreme behavior with Errol bears out this idea—his memories of constant derision and occasional beatings will last a lifetime and cloud his dealings with women.

Instead of nurturing and praising her son, Lily Flynn demands to be the center of attention. So, Errol must work hard to get noticed, and he learns that outrageous or shocking behavior is a way to do it. He will always attempt to shock and will reveal his scars later in life through a cruel streak, particularly when he's drunk.

Lastly, through the derision and beatings at his mother's hand, he acquires two other attributes: self-loathing, that he is never good enough and never right, and distaste for authority. He scorns all figures who might wield power over him, whether teachers or cops or creditors or lawyers or reporters or directors or heads of studios. Errol Flynn will always have to feel like he's autonomous and not under anybody's thumb.

Errol vs. Lily Mary is a strained relationship that fuels a basic conflict about women within Flynn—he is ferociously attracted to the good-looking ones while being unable to trust them; ultimately, he needs to conquer women to mitigate their hold on him. He gravitates to two types of females: older women, who perhaps remind him of Mom, and teenaged girls—the age he never leaves emotionally. For his entire life he returns to girls of 16 or 17 or 18 because that's where his mind is stuck, in adolescence.

Errol does pick up a valuable trait from his mother. He learns that an attractive outward veneer that includes snappy attire, diligent grooming, and a pleasing smile goes far in the world. Even when he is down on his luck in his late teens and into his twenties, and his clothes are threadbare, at first glance he looks like *somebody*.

Lily Flynn also imbues young Errol with charm. World-class charm. World-renowned charm. But it goes only so

far. "He has the charm to lure birds out of the trees if he wishes," will say Florabel Muir, a features writer who knows Errol Flynn the film star very well, "but he can be nasty and disagreeable upon occasion. He has a trigger temper that embroils him in fights and arguments wherever he goes."[3]

His biologist father is an intellectual, quiet and introspective, and Errol absorbs this side too. He becomes an observer of life, looking at people and places with the same intense curiosity with

Lily Mary Flynn, 1913 (John Hammond Moore Collection)

which Theo Flynn would examine a rare specimen, thinking deeply and writing tenderly. The good professor also has a roving eye, and rumors of his flings hang around the university long after the Flynns have departed.

Errol Flynn is the sum of all these parts, well mannered and wild, sensitive and cruel, curious and disdainful. These dichotomies will surprise people all his life. Some combination of these traits will make him wildly successful; others will cause his downfall and early death.

Despite their failings, Lily and Theo Flynn are bright, articulate, and inquisitive people, and Errol grows up smart, absorbing from them a quick mind, ready sense of humor, good vocabulary, and desire for an attractive personal presentation.

He spends his first 17 years in a variety of locations, including England and Australia, but mostly these years find him in Hobart, Tasmania, as "a devil," lazy, undisciplined, and unable to be controlled. He makes an indifferent student who, in 1925 at age 16, ranks 29 in a class of 31.[4]

A classmate provides a telling description of the mid-1920s Errol Flynn, then in his teens: "His character was dominated by a contempt for convention and a desire to shock. He was the complete egotist. His extreme good looks were spoilt by an incredibly smug expression, plainly seen in his pictures."[5]

At age four, Errol Flynn was already a "devil boy." He is photographed in Hobart, Tasmania. (John Hammond Moore Collection)

Actor Basil Rathbone delivers a mirror description of the late-1930s Flynn: "I think his greatest handicap was that he was incapable of taking himself or anyone else seriously.... He was monstrously lazy and self-indulgent, relying on a magnificent body to keep him going, and he had an insidious flair for making trouble, mostly for himself.... It

By the time this photo was taken in Sydney, Australia, 20-year-old Flynn had already spent two years in New Guinea working with little success at a variety of jobs. (John Hammond Moore Collection)

was always 'dear old Bazzz,' and he would flash that smile that was both defiant and cruel, but which for me always had a tinge of affection in it."[6]

Well into adulthood, Flynn is known for being stuck in adolescence. It seems that those who know him can't miss

it. "Errol has never gotten over being 15 years old," says reporter Dan Camp of the Robin Hood-era Flynn.[7] When Flynn *is* 15 years old, he excels in one area: sports—Australian-rules football, boxing, and especially tennis. His build, agility, and hand-eye coordination combine to make him a superior athlete. In a corner of the world where tennis reigns supreme, Flynn becomes a local champion, renowned for powerful ground strokes and confounding placement. But he must rely on the competition of school teams, and by 1927 he has been expelled from, seemingly, every eligible institution of learning in Hobart and Sydney. Out of academic options, he closes this chapter of his life and heads to the goldfields of New Guinea, lured there by the thought of easy money.

Flynn arrives in Rabaul, New Guinea, which writer John Hammond Moore describes as "a raucous, swinging, South Seas whore of a town." Here he becomes a character out of South Pacific fiction—sunburnt, clad in dirty undershirt and captain's cap, chomping a cigar, and playing cards at all hours. He wears out his welcome in job after job; he takes none of them seriously.

Screenwriter Steven Hayes knew Flynn well and helps make sense of the actor's seemingly chaotic actions, as a youth and throughout his life. "With Errol, most things were instant gratification. I don't know whether he had Attention Deficit Disorder. Of course it wasn't called that back then, but if you'd tested him for ADD, I wouldn't be surprised if he'd had it."[8]

As Flynn himself will say as a Hollywood star, "I don't plan my days—I'm ready for whatever happens." His first wife, Lili Damita, will agree: "Oh, he's appalling. He never knows what time it is and doesn't care. He has five watches and never wears or carries one of them."[9]

His second wife, Nora Eddington, will say, "Errol's plans had a habit of changing at the last minute."[10]

Errol Flynn of the South Seas becomes, in short order, a police cadet, assistant manager of a copra plantation, mechanic, cargo clerk, and many other things, but never for long and never successfully. He lasts longest as a "native recruiter," prowling the New Guinea coast looking for able-bodied black men to impress as laborers. But life is so hard in New Guinea that Flynn heads back to Australia, carrying gonorrhea and malaria with him.

Errol Flynn was 23 when he served as a plantation overseer and newspaper correspondent in New Guinea—and began to show the first hint of maturity. (John McElwee Collection)

than, "Mom bought it for me." He and his friends sail *Sirocco* for several months, using her mostly as a platform to get girls. When she hits a reef, Flynn gives up on his sailing career and drifts on.

Next, he tries his hand at running a tobacco plantation and fails, but he gives it his gamest effort to date and begins to show a hint of maturity. He also writes short articles for the Sydney *Bulletin*, revealing a remarkable discipline for the craft of writing, with every word contributing to his theme of the day. His *Bulletin* articles also reflect in print the easy charm that gets him chance after chance in life. And his next chance is a life changer—he is spotted on a beach and offered the role of Fletcher Christian in an independent Australian motion picture documentary called *In the Wake of the Bounty*. Flynn will later admit that he had no idea what to do on a movie set, and the wife of the director recalls that the charming Flynn, in his weeks of work in the picture, "breezed into our lives, caused trouble with the girls in the studio, and left."[11]

Errol Flynn is now only 20 as the calendar goes, but he's already a world-weary, brawling, poker-playing, womanizing petty thief who has tried and failed at literally dozens of jobs. He becomes enamored of a 50-year-old black-hulled yacht named *Sirocco* in Sydney Harbor and wants to buy it. With no funds and no credit, he asks his parents to intervene, and it will be the combative Lily Mary Flynn who writes a check for £120 for the purchase of part interest in the boat in a desperate attempt to help her son discover adulthood. Flynn will tell wild tales about how he came to own the *Sirocco*, all of which sound more romantic

Flynn's acting debut is set among a hodgepodge of antique stage-play interiors and location exteriors. He is lean, and his Aussie accent thick. "We are become self-made villains," he twangs to a fellow mutineer. But it *sounds* like, "We are become self-mide veelins." At the same time, this early celluloid captures the brass of Errol Flynn as he owns the motion picture frame despite no experience in so much as a school play. It is the world's first glimpse of the fearless Flynn.

His new celebrity leads him into a sexual dalliance with a wealthy, sophisticated member of Sydney society. It is a time in his life when a number of Flynn's inner demons meet: the need to conquer older women, the contempt for authority figures, the ability to rationalize disreputable acts. The woman's jewelry turns up missing, and Flynn leaves Australia in haste.

During a stop in New Guinea to pick up cash recruiting natives, he spends downtime at a Lutheran mission on the northern coast and, as is his wont, records his thoughts in a diary. "Coloured prints of Christ are regarding me dolefully from every angle of the room," writes Flynn. "He is portrayed in a large variety of postures.... Why is it that Christ is never shown smiling? He must have laughed sometimes."[12] Flynn takes few things in life seriously, but he will always use his writing to remark on the ironies he sees. He will work hard at writing, and wish to be a writer, and muster all his forces to focus his meandering attention on it. For periods of time, he even will succeed.

It's not clear when or why he sets out for England, except that his father is teaching there, and acting jobs are plentiful. On the passage, Flynn meets a man who will be an important influence on his life, Austrian physician Hermann Erben, a bespectacled, gap-toothed roughneck with a heavy accent who seems to have been straight out of Central Casting; a man every bit as amoral as Flynn. Erben is a photographer; Flynn is a writer. Together they adventure their way west, each recording for posterity the journey toward, for each, a significant life.

Flynn and Erben travel through Asia, the Middle East, and the Mediterranean. That Errol Flynn has escaped the South Seas alive—surviving storm-tossed oceans, tropical diseases, headhunters, and jealous husbands—is proof enough of Flynn's Luck. He is a survivor; he just is, and he knows it.

Flynn and Erben reach Vienna in June 1933, and Flynn goes on to Paris, where he meets French movie star Lili Damita. The multi-lingual Damita has much in common with Flynn's mother, down to their first names. Damita is between five and ten years older than Flynn—she evades all attempts to pinpoint her age—and, like Flynn, a sexual athlete. Older, beautiful, fiery, continental, and openly bisexual, Damita throws Flynn for a loop. In their conversations, when they take a break to actually *talk*, she describes the picture business and gives this exciting young

THE TORTOISE & THE FIRE

By Errol Flynn
Sydney *Bulletin*, January 27, 1932

Killing a turtle in New Guinea is a horribly messy business. I once came upon several natives about to dispatch a 600 lb. specimen. The turtle was lying on its back on the beach, helplessly flapping, and my cook-boy, Mai-Iki, squatted nearby, kindling a fire on its stomach. Bellowing loudly I rushed to the rescue, scattered the fire, and, in honest rage, was about to inflict grievous bodily harm on Mai-Iki. Deciding, however, that he knew no better, I sent a boy for my revolver, and, while awaiting him, discoursed to the assembly on the evil of cruelty to animals. To my annoyance Mai-Iki wanted to debate the matter. "Master," he said earnestly, "this fella he no savvy die quick time. S'pose you shoot 'im he no die." "No?" I said, "you watch," and pumped three rounds from a .32 into its head. To my chagrin the turtle showed no sign of having noticed anything unusual, and did not even interrupt the slow pendulum-like movement of its head from side to side. Rather staggered by such unconcern I fired three more rounds, but with the same result. The thing seemed slightly bored with the proceedings and certainly displayed no resentment. "Bring akis!" (bring an axe) I shouted desperately. "Cut off head belong 'im." That was done and the turtle, I thought, was out of its dreadful agony. But when, to my amazement, the headless body continued to breathe through the severed windpipe, as though losing a head was an everyday occurrence, I threw the towel in. "All right," I told Mai-Iki, "go ahead and kill it anyway you like." He remade the fire and when the tissue was no longer like leather cut the flesh around the edge and removed the stomach shell, leaving the inside exposed. It was such an uncanny sight to see the heart pumping and everything else apparently working to schedule that I repaired to the house for a drink. Even when I returned several hours later the turtle wasn't quite dead.

man the idea that Hollywood should be his final destination. And Hollywood might best be reached via work at the Warner Brothers Teddington Studios.

Flynn finally reaches England in early July for a reunion with his parents—and his sister Rosemary, whom he has never really known. He delights in getting reacquainted with his father, from whom he craves acceptance, but Errol still hasn't made any inroads into growing up and finding a career. He writes a postcard to Erben on July 5, 1933, only two weeks after they had parted company in Vienna: "Dear Doc/Expect letter from me in three or four days' time with an idea for making money using your photos for a lecture tour—my father thinks he can arrange it with some folk who have **cash**—really good money. Send the photos as soon as possible. Hope you're okay? Regards, Errol Flynn"[13]

But before this scheme can amount to anything, Flynn lands a job at Warner Brothers Teddington, appearing as a dancer in a musical starring the dishy Margot Grahame called *I Adore You*, released in November 1933 and now a lost film.

With two celluloid credits to his name, Flynn blusters his way into the Northampton Repertory Theatre, a company that plays London's West End, claiming to be a swimmer in the Olympics, a champion boxer, and star of Australian *and* British films. Fearless Flynn strikes again—he lands a job. The rough-and-tumble lad with bad teeth and that rowdy Aussie accent will spend six months at

ERROL FLYNN

FILMS: Lead in "In the Wake of the Bounty"
—Chauvel Prods. Ltd. (American-Tahiti)
"I Adore You"—Warner Bros. "Third Degree"—B.I.P., etc., etc.

Photos : Sasha.　　　　　　Height 6 feet 1 inch

NORTHAMPTON
REPERTORY
THEATRE

Olympic Games
Boxing Representative

c o "The Spotlight"
GERrard 3002

An ambitious Errol Flynn took out this ad in the British theatre magazine, *The Spotlight*, to trumpet his accomplishments and his promise. Rather than alluding to his considerable (and legitimate) ability as a tennis player, Flynn chose a little hyperbole regarding his boxing skills.

Northampton, smoothing the rough edges and working six days a week—harder than he has worked in his life. He also will live lavishly, employ his indefensible charm on local merchants, and then take care of business as usual, according to author Gerry Connelly, "by running up debts and leaving town before the debts were settled."[14]

This behavior will prove instructive to Errol Flynn a decade later, when he is Master of Mulholland. Connelly speculates that this is Flynn's way of "beating the system," but later, when he's in his physical and monetary prime as a world-renowned movie star, he will still live beyond his means, run up debts, and leave town before the debts are settled. At Northampton, according to Connelly, "Flynn began to spend in anticipation of his wages; then began to ask the theatre for wage advances." The Errol Flynn papers at the Warner Brothers Archives at USC reveal this recurring theme in his years at the studio—in one case, Flynn is paid in 1943 for a feature film that isn't completed and released until 1945!

Errol Flynn's career at Northampton ends abruptly after a night of hard drinking and some bad manners. He rebounds by returning to Warner Brothers Teddington armed with a real-and-fictitious resume, now woven into an impenetrable tapestry of genuine and imagined skills and hard-earned and fanciful credits. Flynn lands the lead in a B-film, catches the attention of Jack L. Warner at the Burbank, California headquarters, and is summoned to America. He arrives at the Port of New York on the SS *Paris* on November 20, 1934. He lists his destination as Warner Bros. Inc., Burbank Studios, Hollywood, Cal., and notes that he plans to stay for six months.[15]

The vivacious Lili Damita, fading silent movie siren, hears Flynn's news and determines that she must latch

Lili Damita's charms are obvious in this European postcard image. Always a leg man and an admirer of older women, Errol Flynn fell immediately, and fell hard, for the pint-sized French movie star who was up to 10 years his senior (no one knew for sure).

onto this rising star. They arrive in America together and get married in Yuma, Arizona. She introduces him to her American friends in the highest strata of Hollywood society. Errol and Lili take up residence together on Appian Way, a narrow, hairpin-curved mountain path located off Laurel Canyon Boulevard in the Hollywood Hills. Flynn lands two small film roles at Warners, and then Flynn's Luck strikes again.

The story of the casting of *Captain Blood*, the studio's epic, million-dollar tale of pirates on the high seas, will be recounted for decades—Jack Warner calls the rookie (Flynn) off the bench and sends him into the game when all the power hitters are unavailable. Less well known is the fact that Lili is pulling strings behind the scenes. Directing *Captain Blood* will be fiery Hungarian Michael Curtiz, who has learned his craft in Europe as both actor and director with movie credits dating back to 1912. The Worldwide Web suggests that Curtiz and Damita had been married in the mid-1920s. At the very least, Curtiz had directed Damita in Europe, and they are well acquainted, giving Lili the perfect opportunity to intervene. She also asks J.L.'s wife for help, although the subterfuge may have been unnecessary—Warner is already intrigued by Flynn.

Flynn is cast as the doctor-turned-pirate and processed through the studio for grooming and publicity. He goes to "star school," gets his teeth capped, and poses for hundreds of still photos frolicking with girls.

At the first set of *Captain Blood* costume fittings, Errol Flynn meets a young ingénue who is also getting the star build-up. "I was called for a test, simply a silent test," recalls Olivia de Havilland, "and they said, 'Would you please stand next to Mr. Flynn?' and I saw him. Oh my! Oh my! Struck dumb. I knew it was what the French call a *coup de foudre*. So I took my position next to him, and I was very, very formal with him because that is the way you were in those days. We had never met...and we just stood there next to each other. Oh!"[16]

On the set of *Captain Blood*, Flynn meets another person who will be important in his life. Tough-as-nails stuntman Buster Wiles quickly becomes one of Flynn's best friends

BY ACTUAL COUNT
A MILLION DOLLARS' WORTH OF ADVENTURE
packed by Warner Bros. into this miracle of motion pictures!

SEE 1500 MEN BATTLING TO THE DEATH WITH CLUB AND CUTLASS

WATCH GIANT SHIPS CRASHING IN COMBAT IN MID-ATLANTIC

SEE THE SLAVE MARKETS OF THE CARIBBEAN REPRODUCED IN ALL THEIR INFAMY

JOIN

MAKING IT WAS THE GREAT ADVENTURE OF THE SCREEN... SEEING IT WILL BE YOURS!

From RAFAEL SABATINI'S world-famed classic—introducing the new star sensations—
ERROL FLYNN
in the role that lured him from London triumphs
OLIVIA DE HAVILLAND
Dream Girl of "A Midsummer Night's Dream"
LIONEL ATWILL • BASIL RATHBONE • ROSS ALEXANDER • GUY KIBBEE • HENRY STEPHENSON • ROBERT BARRAT•
Directed by MICHAEL CURTIZ

A Cosmopolitan Production
A FIRST NATIONAL PICTURE

After watching the rushes, J.L. Warner doesn't mind admitting that he'd made a million-dollar gamble on newcomers Errol Flynn and Olivia de Havilland. This theater giveaway advertises *Captain Blood*, the studio's grand adventure tale of pirates on the high seas.

Newlyweds Errol and Lili Flynn pose for another in a seemingly endless series of publicity photos. Her career has hit the rocks, but she doesn't care because she is living the high life with one of the most famous men in the world. Lili will tell a writer for *Screenland* magazine in 1939, "There are definite advantages in being married to a movie star." Except this movie star sleeps around...*a lot*.

and a central member of his pack. Wiles is a hard-drinking, hard-gambling charmer with a thick Tennessee accent. He invites the quiet Errol to a crap game on the soundstage. "He joined the gambling," says Wiles, "and from that day on, he was one of the guys, quite an admired and well-liked star on the Warner lot."[17] For the next 10 years, the fearless Flynn will rarely be found far from the fearless Wiles.

Captain Blood is the big Warner Brothers release for Christmas 1935, and the Aussie roustabout, the guy who can't keep a job and skips out on his bills, the guy who defies authority figures, suddenly finds himself a

Hollywood star of the first magnitude. It turns out that the very dysfunctions and personality disorders that made Flynn a miscreant on other continents allow him to fit in perfectly in Hollywood, where he becomes the formidable problem of the man in charge at Warner Brothers studio, Mr. Jack L. Warner—perhaps the toughest authority figure Errol Flynn could ever find to bedevil.

As Flynn begins his career, he doesn't know that the most important piece of real estate in his life is just up the mountain from Warners. On a clear day he could even see it—if he knew, that is, where toward the southwest to look.

In 1935, Warner Brothers ordered a series of still photos depicting its new star at home with his loving bride. Here they pose in the Appian Way house. A portrait of Damita by Alberto Vargas was hung above the fireplace, an idea Flynn stored away for future use.

B y the release of *Captain Blood*, Errol Flynn, the movie star exhibiting ADD-like symptoms, is restless in his new marriage. He suffers from a roving eye for women, angering the hot-tempered Damita, whom he has nicknamed "Tiger Lil." His eye also roves for land, and Lili tells a *Screenland* magazine reporter, "He's money-conscious [and] tries to invest carefully, in real estate, insurance, stocks."

Sometime in 1935 Flynn motors up Mulholland Drive, a dusty mountaintop road a couple miles from the house on Appian Way, and on this outing, between Laurel Canyon and Cahuenga, he spots *it*: the piece of land that he must own, with a high hill jutting above to the west, a sheer south-side drop off, and a Boy Scout camp to the east. Facing north is Mulholland Drive, and on the far side of the road, a mountainside that plummets straight down into the San Fernando Valley. It's quiet, secluded, and a touch dangerous; there aren't, and can't be, any neighbors.

It is also historic ground, which Flynn himself notes. "There...the forces of Lt. Col. John C. Fremont engaged in bloody battle with those of Gen. Andres Pico," Flynn writes later, "and routed them as is recorded in the articles of capitulation for the Treaty of Cahuenga, which passed the village of Los Angeles from Mexican to American rule...where Mulholland Farm now stands."[18] How does Flynn know this? He reads it on the grave of James B. Lankershim (1850-1931), who is buried just a few feet beyond Flynn's property line under a 14-foot-tall monument, with plaques telling of notable area events.

Production on his second starring film, *The Charge of the Light Brigade*, is winding down on May 24, 1936, when Flynn writes a check for $527.50 as down payment for this parcel of about eight-and-a-half acres of land along Mulholland Highway. Other Flynn biographers place the purchase of the Mulholland property much later, but Flynn's check to A. Poole on May 24 confirms his 1936 purchase of much of the land that will comprise his estate. He pays $1,185 per acre, for a total price of $9,500.[19] Around this time, he begins writing again and sells Warner Brothers an original screenplay, created with scriptwriter William Ullman, entitled *The White Rajah*. Flynn uses part of the proceeds to fence in his Mulholland property.

Soon he is back making pictures, including *Green Light*, a medical drama with Anita Louise and Margaret Lindsay, and *The Prince and the Pauper*, for which he receives $25,000 to save an otherwise ponderous picture featuring the likeable 15-year-old twin boys, Billy and Bobby Mauch. He then completes *Another Dawn*, a tidy romance of interest today because it pairs him with just his kind of older woman—the studio's glamour queen, Kay Francis.

Flynn is already active at his property, which will be his pet project for the next five years. He cuts a driveway and installs gates and a plank sign reading Mulholland Farm. He builds a caretaker's bungalow on the front corner beside the driveway. He clears and grades what he calls the "lower pasture," and installs a riding ring with jumps, a corral, and runs for animals that include ducks, geese, pheasants, and two wallabies sent to him from Australia.

Here Hermann Erben reenters the picture, putting the idea into Flynn's head that it would be fun to go to Spain to observe the civil war between loyalists and fascists. Hemmed in by his marriage, bored by his relentless 8 a.m. calls, the "monstrously lazy" and fearless Flynn jumps at the chance. In February 1937 he makes a deal to cover the war for Hearst newspapers and skips the country. Warner Brothers protests, but Flynn is already gone. Before he leaves, he hand-writes a page that authorizes his business agent, William Best, to oversee "my properties on Mulholland Highway."[20]

Flynn and Erben experience the Spanish Civil War close up. Reports (perhaps generated by Flynn himself) reach Jack Warner that the star has been killed in the fighting. In truth, Flynn

The elegant Flynns attend the 1936 Academy Awards. Just down the table sits Louella Parsons.

ERROL FLYNN, GLAMOR BOY

MAY 23, 1938 10 CENTS

Flynn was the most famous man in the nation on May 23, 1938, when a Peter Stackpole portrait appeared on the cover of *Life*. The inside spread showed Flynn cavorting on his yacht *Sirocco*.

and Erben spend a great deal of time adventuring, sometimes callously, through a devastated and suffering land, only to return safe and sound in April 1937. Back at work, Errol knocks off the light comedy, *The Perfect Specimen*, with Warner Brothers curvaceous girl-next-door, Joan Blondell.

Errol resumes his husbandly duties on Appian Way, and Errol and Lili limp on as man and wife despite brutal encounters, such as the evening they celebrate their wedding anniversary in a room filled with well-wishers. Flynn arrives an hour late, presumably after nailing some hat-check girl in some quiet corner, and Lili brains him with a champagne bottle. As he crumples to the floor, Flynn decks his diminutive wife with a right cross. Bloody and broken, both require hospitalization. Lili will never forgive him for breaking her tooth, and the couple agree in short order that it would be less lethal to separate.

Whatever his deficiencies as a husband, box-office returns from picture after picture confirm for J.L. that Flynn's got "it." Star power. He's got so much of "it," in fact, that Warner is ready to roll the dice—and Jack L. Warner is loathe to gamble. J.L. gives the go-ahead for Flynn to star in the prestige Warner picture of the year, *The*

Adventures of Robin Hood, a three-strip Technicolor production that will win Academy Awards and make Flynn a household word.

Errol reports for his first makeup, wig, and wardrobe tests on August 13, 1937, and works straight through to mid-January 1938 to complete *Robin Hood*. In that time he makes a serious play for Olivia de Havilland, who is out of fight and ready to give in—until suddenly Damita appears on location to intercept Flynn's forward pass. Lili seems to possess a sixth sense about rivals moving into her territory. In no way will Lili Damita allow a young thing like Olivia de Havilland, not yet 23, to make Damita look bad in the eyes of the public. All Lili has going for her at this point, with her career ended, is her reputation and her very famous husband.

Clearly Lili's strategy to hitch her wagon to Flynn's star is failing. She has seen no career resurgence, and she is known now only as Mrs. Errol Flynn. He, on the other hand, no longer needs Damita to make introductions or further his image. Now, there is only sexual chemistry. "We were poles part," says Flynn, "except in bed. Mentally, woefully inadequate. Sexually, fabulous, wonderfully exciting, beautiful. All this became the source of an irritation that grew and grew."[21]

By 1938 Flynn's income flows in via several streams. In 1937 he had completed his first book, *Beam Ends*, which enjoys impressive success, and he sells several articles to *Photoplay* magazine, including the feature, "What Really Happened to Me in Spain."

Flynn follows up *Robin Hood* with a bad comedy with de Havilland and a mediocre drama with Bette Davis. But then he scores a dramatic triumph with the first film in which he flexes his acting muscles, *The Dawn Patrol*, co-starring David Niven and Basil Rathbone. *The Dawn Patrol* confounds Flynn critics because it doesn't reflect the usual

Fearless Errol Flynn sports a nasty gash after being belted with a champagne bottle by his wife at a party celebrating their anniversary. Fifty witnesses watched Flynn spin, tighten up his fist, and deck Damita before he fell, as they, in effect, knocked each other out. The studio explanation for the cut: Errol was protecting Lili as their car veered off Laurel Canyon Boulevard and struck a wall.

Flynn performance—a charming guy walking through his part. This Flynn fellow just might be an actor after all.

By now, Flynn has moved out of the Appian Way house, and he sets up womanizing operations with Niven at 601 North Linden Drive in quiet Beverly Hills, with a weekend bungalow on the beach in Santa Monica. When he reconciles with Damita, Flynn buys the North Linden house for the two of them. In response to a reporter's question if they're headed for divorce, he snaps, "Go to hell!"[22] He tells another reporter, "I bought some property up on a

Errol Flynn's house at 601 North Linden Drive in Beverly Hills. He lived there with Niven; then he tried to live there with Damita, to no avail.

that they can't keep their hands off each other. But all the while, he is thinking about Mulholland.

Around this time, he purchases the Boy Scout camp next door, raising his holdings to 11 acres.

As 1938 turns to 1939, Errol Flynn embarks on a new film-making odyssey, *Elizabeth the Queen*, which becomes, after machinations by co-star Bette Davis and by Flynn, *The Private Lives of Elizabeth and Essex*. The play by Maxwell Anderson gives Flynn an opportunity to show off what he had learned during the time he had spent at Northampton. Flynn biographers Tony Thomas, Rudy Behlmer, and Clifford McCarty

hilltop so we could build from our own original plans, but I can't afford to start that yet." He and his faithful schnauzer, Arno, take the reporter, Dickson Morley, up to the work site on Mulholland Highway.

Standing at the edge of the shelf where Flynn's house will go, Morley says, "The site was breathtaking," from the valley below to the mountains beyond.

Flynn says proudly that he's got eight acres, all landscaped. "I had some fun investigating all the nurseries in town," he says, "selecting exactly what was appropriate in trees and shrubs and flowers." He points out his tool shed, the area he's had leveled for a tennis court, and the corral. By this time he has already planted bougainvillea and iceplant that will bloom for 45 years.

"There should be a barn here to go with the corral," he sniffs. "Would have been, too, but I refused to be gypped."[23]

Whether or not he is serious in stating that he wants to build with Lili, the Flynn-Damita reunion leads to another split, a process repeated for the next few years. The only thing standing between the Flynns and a divorce is the fact

credit Davis's performance, saying she surmounts an unhappy production, "but with Flynn the enterprise was considerably less than satisfactory. He appeared either uncomfortable, nonchalant, or blithely boyish in many of his scenes with Davis, thus robbing the film of a good deal of credibility."[24]

But the movie-going public of 1939 seems to approve of Warners' bad boy, voting him into the top 10 stars of the most important year in motion picture history, and today, many viewers believe that Flynn's underplaying holds up better than Davis's florid theatricality.

A new decade dawns, and trouble brews on the Burbank lot. Olivia de Havilland, nominated for an Academy Award for her work in *Gone With the Wind*, has now experienced a grown-up production with people like Clark Gable, George Cukor and Victor Fleming, and knows there's a world of filmmaking that transcends the Warner soundstages. Olivia is in a particularly disagreeable mood after being forced into a thankless minor role in *Essex*, and a dusty, miserable ingénue turn in *Dodge City*, both supporting Errol Flynn—who is now openly and nastily stealing scenes by fiddling with things during her lines. Her dissatisfaction impacts Flynn because the studio decides *not* to cast de Havilland in two of his A-pictures of 1940, *Virginia City* and *The Sea Hawk*, or to team Olivia with Errol in a new urbane detective series patterned after William Powell and Myrna Loy's *The Thin Man*. Olivia de Havilland does appear with Flynn in *Santa Fe Trail*, a fictional account of the outbreak of the American Civil War, with Olivia's role rewritten to be more tomboyish and involved. But the trend is downhill for the onscreen lovers, and Flynn's films are suffering as a result.

From Flynn's perspective, why should he care? He's making money at the rate of $6,000 per week in a time when others in America are burning their furniture for heat. By some accounts he hasn't softened much in temperament. Hollywood writer Adela Rogers St. Johns describes the Flynn of these years by noting "his air of rather flippant arrogance."[25]

In 1940, as Flynn hears the siren's call of Mulholland and leads a life of elegant bachelor solitude, Damita slinks in for one final attempt at cohabitation, and Dr. Erben shows up to spend time with the couple. Erben's diary entry of October 30, 1940, indicates that he and Errol had met with an architect to review plans for Mulholland. Erben, an ardent camera buff, takes a series of photos at the construction

site, but the film will be lost while he is in Europe during World War II.

A little more than a week later, on November 9, Erben's diary reads, "Get up late, Errol must love Lily, drive to his ranch, he rides…"[26] Errol may have found his wife oddly different, perhaps a little moodier, a tad plumper, a bit (or a

Flynn and Damita aboard his yacht *Sirocco* during a truce, 1938. "God, they were good looking," said actress Evelyn Keyes in her autobiography. "She had an extraordinary figure that fairly undulated…and Errol Flynn. He was so beautiful it stopped my breath."

Flynn enjoys a day at the beach with his pals, including Patric Knowles (right), who appeared with him in three films, including *The Adventures of Robin Hood*.

the ultimate irony, which he chooses never to write about: In order to build his house, he opts to make monthly alimony payments; in 15 years, the inability to make monthly alimony payments will cost him his house.

The project proceeds slowly, as witnessed by a features writer, Ginny Wood, who periodically visits the Mulholland property. "Many times I had seen it during the initial landscaping and leveling off of the home site. There it had always ended. Time and again, blueprints would appear, were discarded, and new ones begun."[28]

Flynn makes more movies— *Footsteps in the Dark*, the detective picture that had been planned for de Havilland, and *Dive Bomber*, a service drama shot in San Diego that receives the cooperation of

lot) more responsive. The fortyish Lili Damita Flynn is three months pregnant.

In 1941 Flynn and Damita (now noticeably with child) agree to divorce. It is the end of years of love and hate, dominated by loud and sometimes public fights. He describes these battles as "bitter...talk that can twist the guts; when the wits are keen, the language violent and dirty. You do not care. You are hurting each other. You intend to hurt."[27]

After years of discord, the pregnant Lili says with a smile, "Now I have you." And she does, and Flynn doesn't even realize it. He's too busy building his bachelor pad on Mulholland Highway. During legal proceedings, Damita's attorney offers Flynn the option of making a lump-sum payment to settle the divorce. He chooses to make monthly alimony payments instead, figuring that Lili would remarry and his obligation would be ended. By this time he needs cash to offset cost overruns that accompany the ever-changing blueprints for his home under construction. It becomes

the U.S. War Department to show off Navy air power (in Technicolor) to increasingly hostile Axis Powers.

In the summer of 1941 Flynn begins filming the story of fearless, charismatic General George Armstrong Custer— inventor of Custer's Luck. When Errol reads the script, he asks for Olivia de Havilland as his co-star. Olivia is sick to death of the parade of heroine roles, just as she has outgrown the perpetual adolescent Errol Flynn. "I longed to play a character who initiated things," she says, "who...interpreted the great agonies and joys of human experience, and I certainly wasn't doing that on any kind of level of a significance playing the love interest."[29] She's now an accomplished actress who has worked outside of Warner Brothers. So it's a surprise when Olivia reads the Custer script and agrees to participate, to Flynn's delight. Production of *They Died with Their Boots On* will usher in the best year of Errol Flynn's life, and the last really good one, even though he will live on for 18 years, including a decade at Mulholland Farm.

Above: After wrapping *Dodge City*, his first Western, Errol Flynn traveled to Fort Myer, Virginia, in February 1939. There he rode President Franklin Roosevelt's entry in a horse show. With such star power brought to bear, it was no surprise that the president, his horse, and Errol Flynn won an award. Here Flynn poses with FDR at the event, beginning an association that Flynn would cherish for the rest of his life. During his years at Mulholland, he displayed an autographed photo of FDR in a frame beside his desk. An inscribed photo from Eleanor Roosevelt was nearby. (John McElwee Collection)

Left: Long before he began construction of his house, Flynn had accumulated quite a menagerie, which he kept in pens and a barn built on the lower pasture at Mulholland Farm. Here in 1940 Flynn takes a break from production of *The Sea Hawk* to cavort in the pens with a goat just born there and a Rhodesion Lion Hound puppy from the first litter of the breed ever born in the United States. During this period a caretaker living in a bungalow at the edge of the property kept all in order.

The opening of Earl Carroll's Sunset Boulevard nightclub on December 26, 1938, brings out a glamorous group that seems to be having some fun. Rumored bisexual divas Lili Damita and Marlene Dietrich sit at center, with Lili clutching saucy Ann Boyer Warner, wife of J.L. Jack shares a laugh with Flynn, who eyes the line of lovelies.

Watch those hands, Flynn! Errol admitted to having the hots for Jack Warner's wife Ann, who was at this time carrying on a wild affair with Eddie Albert that would end Albert's Warner Brothers career. Here Ann and Errol dance at Earl Carroll's grand opening.

MULHOLLAND HIGHWAY

The winding, dramatic Mulholland Highway, including Mulholland Drive, traverses the Santa Monica and San Fernando Mountains for nearly 50 miles, running west all the way to the Pacific Ocean, largely on land once held by Isaac Lankershim—brother of James B. (who was buried a few feet from Flynn's property line). In 1909, Isaac Lankershim sold 47,500 acres of land to developers Harrison Grey Otis and Harry Chandler for $2.5 million. The lower portions, all prime real estate, would eventually be subdivided to become communities, such as North Hollywood. The rugged terrain in the mountainous areas would see little development. This land was sold off mostly for small ranches.

When the Southern California land boom hit in the early 1920s, land owners in the Hills pushed for a ridgeline road to be constructed that would open up the area, encourage development, and increase property values. On December 27, 1924, a portion of the two-lane dirt and gravel Mulholland Highway was dedicated and opened up for public use. It was named in honor of Civil Engineer William Mulholland (1855-1935), hailed as a visionary for bringing water to Los Angeles and for envisioning the mountaintop highway, and labeled a villain by some for his part in the Saint Francis Dam disaster, which claimed more than 500 lives.

Development along Mulholland was slow and land values remained stagnant. Unlike the lush farmlands in the Valley, property along Mulholland was vulnerable to washouts and mudslides. Wildfires were also a common problem. To this day, sections of Mulholland Drive remain untamed for these reasons.

The isolated estates along Mulholland Drive have provided both shelter and seclusion to many of Hollywood's greats, including Jack Nicholson, Marlon Brando, and Martin Scorsese. But as the narrow ravines and isolated cul de sacs promote privacy, so do the winding roadway and hairpin turns continue to lure hotrodders and racers to this day.

Construction of Mulholland Highway was a manpower-intensive enterprise in 1931.

In 1940, at the height of his popularity, Errol Flynn poses with his leading lady of the moment, Brenda Marshall, in this scene from *The Sea Hawk*. He should have been gazing at Olivia de Havilland, but she had grown weary of these mindless heroine roles. Flynn thought Marshall a suitable and very sexy replacement, but her insecurity and tantrums ultimately doomed her in Hollywood—except as Mrs. William Holden, a role she played for 30 tempestuous, unfaithful, booze-soaked years. Flynn was making a solid three pictures a year at this time and taking home six grand a week, enough to finance the bachelor's paradise he was planning up on Mulholland Drive.

Just a year before his death, Errol Flynn would state in *My Wicked, Wicked Ways*, "She went up fast, like the sails of a boat." And in a single sentence, as he sits in Jamaica at the end of his life and reminisces, Errol Flynn reveals pure love for his lost home, Mulholland Farm.

Finally ground is broken. The house does indeed go up fast—after he decides that no one can capture Errol Flynn's ideas for design better than Flynn himself. He claims that a sea captain's home in Tasmania inspires the look of the house. *Architectural Digest* will refer to it as "…basically 'Connecticut farmhouse,'" while most others will call it a "California colonial." The solid wood-frame structure features diagonal earthquake blocking on all external walls. At 4,000 square feet, it's not a grand Hollywood mansion like those of his contemporaries. It's more on the order of Gable and Lombard's cozy ranch off to the west in Encino. It is his refuge, with a public entrance up the driveway off Mulholland and a private back entrance. If fans are lining the driveway, or too many pals and hangers-on are partying at Mulholland, Flynn can drive along a firebreak skirting the edge of his property and pull in at the back of the house, far from prying eyes.

The parcel sits just 4.6 miles up the mountain from the Warner Brothers Studios, and presents a panoramic view of Burbank and the San Fernando Valley to the north and the breathtaking peaks of the San Gabriel Mountains beyond.

Today, this stretch of Mulholland Drive is as settled as it can be, with million-dollar homes walled off fortress-like behind barricades and fences and shrubs and hedges, all under the watchful eyes of cameras and sensors. But in 1941 Flynn has only coyotes for neighbors, which is why he builds here in the first place.

Flynn takes Buster Wiles to the site. "We strolled through the partially completed house, with Errol pointing out the living room and so on. Since I was now single, Errol kindly invited me to live at Mulholland Farm. Until it was thoroughly finished, we lived at Bruce Cabot's residence."[30]

A September 1941 accounting places the construction cost for Mulholland house somewhere around $20,000.[31] The exterior is masonry over wood frame, with a first floor that features one-story wings angling in at 45 degrees off the two-story main section. Second-floor dormers nestle in the pitched shingle roof. The pinched wings hug a flagstone patio and a narrow strip of grass, beyond which sits a swimming pool.

It's the kind of house more likely to be found in Santa Monica or Malibu, on a ledge above the sea, and it's no wonder. The design of the place and its appointments date back to Flynn's youth and visits to his mother's side of the family, the Youngs. They were seafaring people, and they brought the sea home with them in décor.

The west side of the house features the kitchen, butler's bedroom, and three-car garage; a formal dining room is set off in the west wing, with windows comprising two walls and ceiling-to-floor mirrors lining the fourth. A disappearing door leads to a vestibule that connects dining room and kitchen. Under the stairs is a formal bathroom, designated *Men* on the door.

The interior of the main section reflects its owner. A long living room paneled entirely in California pickled pine

This view of the front wall of the den looks through the living room to the edge of the spiral staircase. This deconstruction photo from August 1987 harkens back to the house much as Flynn would have seen it in September 1941 when the walls were going up. Note the horizontal blocking on the studwork, and the sheer wall construction for protection against earthquakes. (Jack Marino Collection)

dominates the downstairs and offers a view of the pool through a north-facing wall packed with windows and French doors. A formal fireplace trimmed with polished brass panels sits opposite the windowed wall. Inset book and curio shelves and beamed pine ceilings complete a rustic and refined look. On the wall to the right of the fireplace hangs a Gauguin; on the wall to the left a Van Gogh. Flynn claims this painting was smuggled out of Holland by Van Gogh's physician, one step ahead of the Nazis. Flynn also states that Hermann Goering himself was after the painting, which made its way to Mulholland via South America.[32]

"Funny thing," says Flynn. "I forgot to build an entrance."[33] He will enter the house through the garage during his years here; others will use the door beside the dining room as the main entrance.

Beside the living room stands a curved bar, designed by Flynn and bound in burgundy Moroccan leather, with inset tiles hand-glazed by Goya. On the wall above the bar hangs a "grotesque and gory" mural of a bullfight painted by celebrity illustrator Henry Clive, who painted one-eyed director Raoul Walsh in among the spectators. Behind the bar is a bathroom, with a designation on the door reading *Ladies*.

The bar holds more than liquor bottles. As revealed by Bob Lindsay, Stuart Hamblen's grandson, and Matthew and Gunnar Nelson, Rick Nelson's sons, the wall behind Flynn's bar contains what Bob Lindsay remembers as "a secret door as high as the bar and all the way to the floor." It opens directly into a cramped triangular sitting room with a view through another two-way mirror into the women's bathroom.[34] It is Flynn's first voyeuristic device, pre-dating his infamous two-way ceiling mirror by several years.

But there are other secret devices as well, like two viewing tubes flush with the ceiling—one in the foyer between the living and dining rooms and the other above the bar—that allow Flynn to peer down from the second floor at activity going on below.

The view from Flynn's walk-in closet shows the fireplace in the master bedroom (the panel beside the fireplace contained a secret staircase to the first floor) and, beyond, stud walls for the second and third upstairs bedrooms. At the far end, the balcony above the garage can be seen faintly. Sheer-wall earthquake bracing is visible in the wall at right. Flynn was careful to include this feature throughout the house. This 1987 photo was taken after removal of the plaster walls. (Jack Marino Collection)

Beyond the bar sits the east wing, which features a den, also in pickled pine with beamed ceiling. Windows dominate the den walls on three sides, broken only by a fireplace in the east wall. Flynn flush mounts speakers inside the walls, and he builds in bookshelves, along with display cases for ship models and guns. One of the cases is backed with a map of San Diego Harbor, where he often sails the *Sirocco*. The inspiration for these features is the Young family. Flynn's mother's brother, Harry, had traveled the breadth of the Pacific. Author John Hammond Moore visited Harry's son, Flynn's first cousin, in the 1970s, and saw, "substantial evidence of those travels—intricate Chinese carvings, spears from the Solomon Islands, ship models, and other mementos of a life spent on the high seas."[35]

In the back corner of his den, Flynn places a leather-topped desk; opposite, in the front corner, he places a burgundy leather chair that matches the bar. In this room Errol will answer fan mail, read scripts, run his lines, write his second novel, *Charlie Bow-Tie Comes to America*, gaze out at mountains in two directions, and sleep some nights. Nearby is the bathroom designated for Ladies (when he's throwing a party), but this is Flynn's bathroom when he's home alone. In the back of the house he builds a steam room featuring tiled caricatures of portly gentlemen and buxom babes.

The nautical theme continues with the staircase to the second floor—a wide spiral that ascends from near the dining room. In the ceiling at the top of the stairwell, Flynn sets a recessed light—another of the forward-thinking features. The second floor is maze-like and uninteresting compared to the first, as if Flynn's attention wandered before completion of the project.

At the top of the stairs, the visitor is faced with a series of doors leading to bedrooms and closets. A large guest bedroom with an adjoining bath sits to the left of the stairs. Beneath this bedroom is the garage. Another smaller bedroom, adjoining the guest bathroom and a powder room, sits above the vestibule. A hallway connects the stairs with Flynn's master bedroom. On either side of the hallway run expansive closets for Flynn's clothing and shoes.

The master bedroom above the living room is a roomy 18 x 17 and features paneled walls and a fireplace that shares the chimney with the fireplace below. Flynn builds a secret staircase into the wall beside the fireplace for quick entrances and escapes via the back of the house. One wall is recessed for the headboard of Errol's bed. He places in-wall speakers above the bed and on the opposite wall, both connected to the radio/record player in the living room.

Adjoining the bedroom is a walk-in closet as large as the second guest bedroom; adjacent to the closet is the master bath, featuring a walk-in shower and a ceramic tile countertop. A 6 x 36-inch stainless steel space heater built into the wall protects against cold California mornings.

Other features adorn the newly completed Mulholland Farm. Beyond the pool, twin stone white lions guard a wrought-iron gate that leads to brick steps descending to a

Flynn and de Havilland appear in the last scene they would shoot together, the parting of the Custers in *They Died With Their Boots On*. Just 4.6 miles away, Mulholland Farm was being painted and furnished. He moved in less than a month later. (John McElwee Collection)

tennis court on the lower plateau. And this tennis court isn't just for show; it's designed for the professional—wide beside the doubles lines and deep behind the baselines, with a high plywood backboard on the east wall for practicing groundstrokes, chain link fence and netting all around, and a patio gallery set into the hillside above. In coming years, the greats of Hollywood and professional tennis will play here.

Below the house Flynn constructs a small, circular, plank-floored building of pickled pine inside and out, with tile work completed at the same time as the steam room. He dubs this building "the casino." Here, for a decade, he will host poker tournaments and stage cockfights until the floor is stained with blood. An interior wall of the casino includes a teller window for betting. In the casino, a stack of folding director's chairs and a collapsible table are at the ready, in case some game or other breaks out.

The square stable next door has capacity for up to six horses. Here he keeps Onyx, the black stud that appears in his movies, along with Little Fella, a former racehorse. They exercise in the ring a little higher in the hill. In the early days of the Farm, Flynn keeps goats, chickens, swans, and a monkey named Chico, who careens across the property dressed in formal attire—including a top hat.

Late in 1941 Mulholland Farm is alive with activity. Wiles serves as Flynn's driver and de facto bodyguard. Flynn hires away from best friend Freddy McEvoy a small, bald, devilish manservant named Alexander Pavlenko, about 35 years of age, with an impenetrable Russian accent, who becomes overseer of the new house. Alex has two vices: gambling and women. He soon discovers that one of the fringe benefits of working for Errol Flynn is "leftovers"—girls Flynn doesn't have time for; girls Flynn stiffs when a better opportunity comes along; girls who come to the house willing to do *anything* to meet Errol Flynn. "Beautiful women came to Mulholland like bees to honey," says Buster Wiles.[36] High up on the mountain, in Errol Flynn's newly completed home, Pavlenko and Wiles find heaven.

Flynn hires two women as well: a French cook named Marie, and 18-year-old Mary Ann Hyde, late of Beverly Hills High School, who serves as his secretary. Young, tall, dark, willowy Mary Ann Hyde has the legs of a dancer, which suits Flynn just fine. A sometimes live-in at Mulholland, Hyde dates him even before the divorce from Lili is finalized. Lastly, Flynn hires an Armenian caretaker dubbed Mr. George to live in the bungalow at the entrance to the driveway and tend the 11 acres of property.

Mulholland Farm is now in operation and as complex as its owner, equal parts writer's refuge, brothel, working farm, and sportsman's paradise. Flynn intends to live out his career here, and he might have, except for one night when the cops come calling and for one angry and highly motivated ex-wife.

Russian expatriate Alex Pavlenko (left) is Flynn's "man" at Mulholland, valet, bartender, and caretaker of the house. Alex also accounts for Flynn's "leftovers," the girls that the Master of Mulholland doesn't have time to accommodate. Here he poses with writer and producer Mark Hellinger behind Flynn's bar during a 1945 party. (Deirdre Flynn Collection)

Right: This was Errol Flynn's poolside view of the Warner Brothers soundstages to the northeast in the San Fernando Valley below Mulholland Farm. Flynn was under contract there for 17 years, 11 while living at Mulholland. In the towering Stage 16 at center, he had worked on *The Sea Hawk* and *Gentleman Jim*. (Photograph by Robert Matzen)

Below: Late in 1941, the sod was laid, the pool was filled, and Mulholland was ready for occupants. Mr. Flynn had built his dream house. This view shows a modest country home that could have been found in Connecticut, near that of Mr. Blandings, rather than Southern California. For a year, Flynn lived here literally and figuratively on top of the world. However, few knew, including Warner Brothers, that the swashbuckler often hid in this mountaintop retreat, paralyzed by depression and unable to work. (John McElwee Collection)

Left: Flynn's research into landscaping led him to place bougainvillea and ice-plant around his property in great abundance. It continued to blossom at the site for 45 years. (Photo by Robert Matzen)

Below: A rare photograph of the elaborate pickled-pine casino in foreground, where cockfights and poker tournaments were held for a decade. Stuart Hamblen relegated the casino to storage. During the Nelson years, Gunnar and Matthew would play around the creepy building but never stray inside. (Photo by Robert Florczak)

Avid legman Errol Flynn chose 18-year-old Beverly Hills High grad Mary Ann Hyde, his girlfriend of the moment, to serve as his secretary in the early days of Mulholland Farm. Among her duties was typing Flynn's novel with the working title, *Charlie Bow-Tie* or *The Show-Off*. By the time of the rape trial, singer-dancer Hyde was making a brief appearance as a circus performer in Universal Pictures' *Flesh and Fantasy*. In the book *Errol and Me,* Nora Eddington, Flynn's new flame, said of his old flame, "I met Mary Ann Hyde. This girl was simply ravishing. 'How can Errol ever want to date me?' I thought. Alongside of her figure mine doesn't seem to belong to a woman." Below, Mary Ann Hyde poses with blonde June Lang and one lucky monkey, while at right she balances deftly on a trapeze—no small feat in three-inch heels. Both photos were taken to promote *Flesh and Fantasy*. Hyde would end her career as a Goldwyn Girl just a year later, in 1944.

Above: Flynn at a charity tennis match in summer 1940. After a successful juniors career in Australia, Flynn brought his tennis game to America. He was a founding member of the West Side Tennis Club in Santa Monica and became the singles champion of all Hollywood. Writer Dickson Morley witnessed a Flynn match at the club and said, "Errol wielding a racket is as satisfying a sight as Errol piercing a Rathbone in a hot dueling shot. He does everything with such terrific enthusiasm and skill. Between sets he'd relax briefly; then he was aceing his opponent again."[37] Tennis suited the swashbuckling side of Flynn perfectly as he marauded through the West Side Club with other Hollywood stars like Gilbert Roland and the rough-edged Carole Lombard. Through Lombard, Flynn met Alice Marble, winner of five Grand Slam singles tournaments. Marble operated the pro shop at the club, and in her book *Courting Danger*, she remembered the day Flynn and his posse pushed their way in and Flynn loudly proclaimed to her that he needed a jockstrap, size large. "I blushed," she said, to the delight of Flynn's crowd. Newsreels of the day captured Flynn's style and grace on the court. He worked at his tennis as hard as he ever worked at anything and became good enough to appear often in celebrity tournaments with Bill Tilden and other pros without ever embarrassing himself. His regulation court at Mulholland included a plywood side wall for practicing and a patio above for spectators.

Said Nora Eddington of the Flynn of 1943: "Every Sunday Mulholland Farm became an open house...girls in droves and tennis players came. They came to laugh, to watch tennis, to free-load. Errol played an excellent game of tennis. Had he concentrated solely upon it experts predicted he could have gained a national ranking."[38]

Above: Flynn had few rivals on Hollywood tennis courts and could always count on leading man Robert Stack for a good match. Here Stack, who had been a national skeetshooting champion, shows off his backhand at Mulholland.

Right: Flynn accessed his tennis court from a set of brick stairs near the pool that connected the upper plateau with the lower part of the property, including the court. A pair of white stone lions guarded the head of these stairs. (Photo by Robert Matzen)

lynn's two-way mirror in the downstairs bedroom, part of the 1945 addition of a new east wing to the house, became the worst-kept secret in Hollywood.

Above the mirror was the attic, accessible through a crawlspace from one of the upstairs bedrooms and by an outside stairway. In the attic a trap door lifted up, revealing the see-through mirror. Flynn claimed that only Bruce Cabot fell victim to the two-way mirror as he made love to a girl on the bed below. Cabot was not amused.

But Hedy Lamarr admitted in her book, *Ecstasy and Me,* that she looked down from the attic through the two-way mirror as an "Italian movie star" changed into her bathing suit.

Actor Robert Douglas, Flynn's co-star in two pictures, was another who succumbed to a look through the two-way mirror. He recalled being at the trap door "which overlooked the fascinating bedroom...in which were a young couple, asleep.... [Flynn] said, 'Watch this; it'll be fun.' We had our champagne; [he] pressed a button. The end right opposite the bed, a screen came up, which woke them up. They both sat up in bed; of course they were naked. He pressed another button, and onto the screen came a pornographic movie. They were so shocked; these two, they sat there and watched.... We went down to the bar and left them there."[39]

In March 1955, *Confidential* magazine broke the news of Flynn's magic mirror to the nation. Flynn sued the magazine and settled out of court for $15,000—but he did not contest the existence of the mirror. Rather, he sued because the magazine said he had abandoned his bride, Pat Wymore, on their wedding night to visit a prostitute.

Above: The only known photo of the trap door in the attic was snapped in 1988. Imagine Flynn and all the famous people who peered down through this porthole. Note that the pane of two-way glass had been removed. (Jack Marino Collection) Below: The ceiling of mirrors in the bedroom as seen in June 1987. Visible at center is the infamous two-way mirror, with deterioration caused by attic heat.

The area with the two-way mirror became Rick Nelson's bedroom—he joked about it on national television with David Letterman. But few outsiders knew about another secret passageway leading from behind the bar to a small viewing area beside the downstairs ladies' bathroom. "There was enough room," says Bob Lindsay, grandson of Stuart Hamblen, "for one or two guys to sit there. Just a small little room. The one wall inside the bathroom was all mirrors—a bathtub and mirrors." Through this pane of two-way glass beside the bathtub, Flynn and his cronies could see and hear *everything* that went on. Flynn claimed in *My Wicked, Wicked Ways* that he bugged the women's bathroom, presumably with a wire-and-speakers setup courtesy of gaffers from the studio. An unlikely confirmation of the bugging device came from Rolling Stones guitarist Ron Wood, who toured the house in the 1970s with an eye for buying it from the Hamblens. "Errol had...two-way mirrors, speaker systems in the ladies' room. Not for security. Just that he was an A-1 voyeur."[40]

Hedy Lamarr also alluded to the spied-upon bathroom in *Ecstasy and Me*, and told of attending one of Flynn's 1949 parties for MGM personnel. "I knew Errol's house well," said Hedy. While driving to the party, she warned the female friend accompanying her, "Many of the bathrooms have peepholes or ceilings with squares of opaque glass through which you can't see out but someone can see in. So be careful."

The secret passageway accessible from the bar, according to Gunnar and Matthew Nelson, continued past the ladies' room and into the stream room, accessed by another trap door below the bench. Said Gunnar Nelson with a touch of glee, "Errol Flynn was a major perv!"[41]

THE GREATEST   SHOW ON EARTH....

Errol Flynn | and his two-way mirror!

Pressed duck wasn't the only thing he served under glass in his wacky house on Mulholland Drive. Some of the other entrees made guests shriek — and head for the nearest bar for a quick bracer!

IT WAS SCARCELY A COUPLE OF HOURS since blonde and lovely Pat Wymore had walked down the aisle with Errol Flynn. The beautiful bride was in an upstairs bedroom of her new husband's home in Beverly Hills, shaking the rice from her hair when there came a soft knock at the door.

Blushing prettily, Pat danced over and threw it open to find her mate of some 120 minutes resplendent in white tie and tails, with a fresh boutonniere in his lapel.

Bowing low, the dashing Mr. Flynn kissed his wife's wrist and expressed the hope that she'd enjoy a good night's sleep. Before the wedding, Pat had dated Errol long enough to know she had an inspired nut on her hands, but this was too much for even her cast-iron aplomb.

"How do you mean, 'get a good night's sleep'?" she gasped. "And, if I'm not being too inquisitive, where are you going?"

The suave hero of a hundred melodramas attempted one more bow and nearly sprawled at her feet. Recovering hastily, he leered significantly at his spanking new spouse.

"I, my dear, am going out to keep a dinner date," he muttered thickly. With that, Flynn zig-zagged down the steps and out the front door of his mansion on Mulholland Drive. He was off to dine and spend the rest of the night—with a call girl.

The incident was novel, to be sure, but only to the new Mrs. Flynn. For in the years before Errol beat it to Europe to escape tax and alimony difficulties, he built up a legend about himself and the midnight frolics in his home that made his swashbuckling heroics on the screen seem like the antics of the Bobbsey Twins.

There was, for instance, the night some months after his marriage to Miss Wymore, when she kicked up her spirits at a party and started dancing for their guests. Pat is no slouch with her heels and toes and had the assembly hypnotized, which may have been too much for the ham in Flynn.

Scene Was Better Than a Minsky Finale

At any rate, Errol—better known to his friends as "the Baron"—suddenly ran out into the middle of the floor with fire in his eye and began to tear off his wife's clothes. Pat broke for safety, yelping in alarm, as Errol staggered after her. The scene was better than a Minsky finale.

Other nights, he turned producer and showed his guests movies of himself and former girlfriends in non-musical comedies that would make the entire Johnston office faint. One starred Errol and a willowy hoyden in nude romps through a tropical garden, and another was an underwater ballet in the seas off Jamaica which had the fish calling for an encore.

But Errol really scaled the heights with dinner parties that Emily Post could chew on for a lifetime. His favorite function of this type spotlighted pressed duck on the table and fresh squabs around it. The duck he presumably got from his butcher. The quails were invariably vice dollies, culled from long lists he kept in an assortment of little black books.

Flynn's weakness for the play-for-pay babes was well nigh incredible, even for Hollywood. He used to order them up not one, two or even three at a time but in coveys of 10, 15 and 20 at a brace.

Some were there to entertain him. Others, as it turned out, were present strictly to enjoy the fun when he staged such practical jokes as allowing his guests to watch through an elaborate peephole while a pal cut capers with one of the daily-for-dough dames.

The fact that he was presenting his buddies in such real-life one act plays might never have come to light had not one of the victims—in this case Bruce Cabot—gotten wise to the stunt.

Errol had a majestic bedroom which he seemed only too willing to loan out to tried and true associates at a moment's notice. Most of them jumped at *(Continued on page 51)*

Flynn walked out on pretty third wife Pat Wymore (left) on bridal night . . . He had a previous date with a play-for-pay babe.

Errol's fun-loving pal Bruce Cabot (right) was victim of trick looking-glass until he got wise, turned the tables on Flynn.

For Flynn, the edge of darkness was at hand, and it was more than the title of his latest picture. As biographer Tedd Thomey observed in his book on the swashbuckler, "The way he lived it was inevitable that he would be clobbered." Here Flynn poses on location with Ann Sheridan during production of *Edge of Darkness* in September 1942.

The Golden Age motion picture industry is an out-growth of the Great Depression. Wealth pours into southern California as if the country has been tipped left and shaken, and all its loose change has jangled there. MGM in Culver City reigns as the grandest of the picture factories, with stars Joan Crawford, Clark Gable, and Judy Garland. Other major studios are less prosperous, such as Columbia, RKO, and Paramount in Hollywood and Universal, which sits just over the hill from the Warner sound stages. Warner Brothers Picture Company is as brash and ambitious as its supreme leader, Jack L. Warner, known simply as J.L., and possesses a stable of talent that includes Flynn, James Cagney, Humphrey Bogart, and multiple Academy Award-winner Bette Davis. And unfortunately for J.L., his stars are a troublesome gang. Olivia de Havilland complains about her limiting "heroine" rolls. Cagney wants a raise and script approval and goes on sus-pension. Bogart grouses about everything and brawls with his wife. Davis is a bitchy prima donna. And Flynn is a god-damn reckless fool—J.L. never knows if his swashbuckler is going to fall off a boat or catch another dose of the clap.

Movie stars are running amok in what now is known as Tinseltown. Bedhopping is rampant, and one-upsmanship supreme. Who has the biggest car, the finest clothes, the best-looking mate, and the choicest home? Movie stars live in palatial mansions in Brentwood, Beverly Hills, or Bel Air.

Or along Mulholland Drive, high atop the Hollywood Hills. Falcon's Lair. Pickfair. The House of the Two Gables. And from these lofty perches, the stars swoop down to a variety of nightclubs clustered about Sunset Boulevard,

most notably the Sunset Strip. The stately Trocadero is the hub of Strip activity. Nearby is Flynn's favorite, the elegant Club Mocambo, where the star had downed gossip colum-nist Jimmy Fidler with one swing in September 1941 for writing unkind remarks about Flynn after the death of his sidekick, the schnauzer Arno. In this incident, Fidler's comely wife Bobby had grabbed the nearest weapon, a salad fork, and famously and bloodily stabbed Flynn in the ear, but such are the raucous times that all became friends and laughed about it later.

Flynn has a hand in other Hollywood nightspots. He is one of many celebrity backers (others include Fidler, Bob Hope, Bing Crosby, and Fred MacMurray) of the Pirate's Den on North La Brea Avenue in Hollywood, a riotous nightclub that flies the Jolly Roger. The wait staff abduct female patrons and perform movie-style stunts in full pirate costume. It perfectly suits Errol Flynn. Other haunts of the star with the wicked ways include Romanoffs on Rodeo Drive in Beverly Hills and Earl Carroll's on Sunset Boulevard near Vine Street, where he routinely has his eyes and hands on the endless parade of showgirls.

Flynn continues to play unabated, while his work is plagued by health problems. On location for *They Died With Their Boots On*, Flynn claims smoke inhalation and misses 11 days of work, incurring $1,599 in hospital bills (which he has sent to the studio for payment).[42] This incident leads to a number of later medical complaints that Flynn will tie to this first illness—which, he is always quick to point out, had been contracted in the line of duty. Soon thereafter, he

It was the first, and the wildest and most wicked, legend attached to Errol Flynn's Mulholland home, and a story so fantastic and with so many eyewitnesses that there has to be truth in it. As late as December 1982, Orson Welles was regaling Johnny Carson with the tale on the *Tonight Show*. A tale that goes like this...

Errol Flynn loved John Barrymore like a wayward uncle, and in the last year of his life, the Great Profile lived in the aqua bedroom for what Flynn called "the most frightening three weeks I had since I was in the New Guinea jungle."[43]

They led similar lives, Barrymore and Flynn, from sailing yachts to quoting the classics, from constant drinking to rampant womanizing, from behavior that was intended to shock to referring to friends and lovers by pet names. When Barrymore succumbed to his excesses on May 29, 1942, at age 60 (but looking a decade older), Raoul Walsh claimed to be visiting Mulholland when John Decker brought the news.

According to Flynn in his autobiography and Walsh in his, the one-eyed director and some drunken friends stole Barrymore's body from venerable Pierce Brothers Mortuary on Sunset Boulevard, located 15 minutes from Mulholland Farm, and took it for a drive. Actor Paul Henreid in his memoirs claimed to be an accomplice. An unsuspecting Alex, said to be smashed when the giggling ghouls arrived, helped Walsh carry Barrymore inside. Alex said he never saw Barrymore so intoxicated. They propped the body on the couch just in time for Flynn to return from an impromptu wake at a local bar.[44]

Flynn claimed they placed Barrymore's body in his favorite chair (presumably the leather chair from the den) in the living room. Walsh said he and Alex propped it up on the sofa (presumably the floral print in the living room). Flynn said, "The lights went on and my God—I stared into the face of Barrymore! His eyes were closed. He looked puffed, white, bloodless. They hadn't embalmed him yet."[45]

Flynn "let out a piercing scream," said Walsh, "and ran out of the house. I went to the doorway and saw Errol standing behind a big oleander bush. When he saw me, he yelled, 'Get him out of the house, you crazy Irish bastard, before I have a heart attack.'"[46]

This story simply won't go away. Yes, it was against the law to move bodies around in the night, but when did that ever stop the denizens of Hollywood, especially a legendary director, one of Hollywood's more powerful men, who was used to having his own way? *Especially* if he was drunk; *especially* if he was out with his pals, also drunk. How was an original Pierce Brother going to defend *that* hill against Raoul Walsh over the remains of a seedy reprobate the likes of John Barrymore? Flynn, Walsh, and crew never let the law stand in the way of a caper, especially if it might produce a genuine heart attack.

"They took him *someplace*," said actor Harve Presnell, a man well-connected around town. "I know that for a fact. They decided to have a wake. They went down to the mortuary and got Jack...and took him wherever they took him. Rigor had set in. They bent him around, stuck him in a chair, and all got shit-faced while he had a drink in his hand, then took him back to the mortuary. That's a true story."[47]

No one knows for sure if Barrymore's last road trip was to Mulholland Farm, a place he had recently visited in life. Friend and biographer Gene Fowler claimed to have spent the night with the body (which seems odd—did he expect a resurrection?). Who says Fowler wasn't trying to protect Barrymore's memory by claiming the body *didn't* go on tour? Buster Wiles claimed that Walsh made up the whole thing. Wiles said it was his idea to steal the body, but he was only joking. In fact, in his book *My Days with Errol Flynn*, Wiles places himself dead center in the Hollywood scene, with stars and executives treating him as an equal and not merely as a stuntman and Flynn hanger-on. In other words, Wiles is not always the most credible source.

Knowing these guys, their disregard for authority and their Olympic drinking (see Chapter Eight regarding a mountain of vodka bottles found in the ravine behind Flynn's den in 1959), the Barrymore body snatching probably happened just the way Flynn, Walsh, Paul Henreid, and Orson Welles said it did.

refuses to report for his next picture, *Forced Landing* (later *Desperate Journey*), because of a sinus infection. The same month he is suspended for four days for his conduct—but later charms studio production manager T.C. "Tenny" Wright into paying the docked salary.[48]

Just as Flynn is moving into his new home, the Japanese bomb Pearl Harbor, sobering up the film community. Six weeks later Hollywood is stunned when the first star dies in the war—vivacious Carole Lombard goes down with her plane as she returns to California from a war bond tour to Indiana. Lombard's husband Clark Gable and pilot Jimmy Stewart lead a long line of matinee idols who enlist in the armed forces.

Bright and early on a Monday morning, February 2, 1942, Buster Wiles drives Flynn to the Selective Service Board, and both take their physical exams for military service. Flynn is turned down by the Army due to a heart murmur and a second diagnosis that takes him by surprise: tuberculosis. Just three days later, Warner Brothers files an Occupational Deferment form, making it clear that their highly bankable star must not be taken away. Question 7 asks for an accurate and full description of his duties. A Warner Brothers representative states, "Registrant is a highly skilled motion picture actor whose services are unique and whose duties consist of portraying roles assigned to him in connection with numerous motion pictures produced by his employer."[49] Just as Flynn tries to serve—and

he makes repeated attempts to be accepted into service only to be turned down because of his heart, TB, and recurrent malaria—Warner Brothers is working behind the scenes to protect its interests.

The public can only be confused, as Flynn is seen in photos and newsreels playing two hours of tennis at a stretch, or sailing, or swimming and diving off his boat, or drinking and carousing past dawn whenever he pleases. Buster Wiles says of Flynn's tuberculosis, "…as serious as the disease was, he didn't go to pieces. It was not an advanced case but Errol did begin resting more."[50] Flynn isn't shy about using his maladies when studio authority figures (J.L. Warner, Hal Wallis, Tenny Wright, and other bosses) make demands that he considers unreasonable.

While on a day shoot at Calabasas near the end of production on *Forced Landing*, just a month after the TB diagnosis, Tenny Wright and Flynn cross swords over quitting time. Flynn wants to knock off at five o'clock. Wright says that they're on location and must work "…as long as the light is good—until six o'clock." Flynn replies that he's a sick man, "…and if you don't believe so, look up the army record." He says he's already going the extra mile by working until five o'clock when he's bushed. Wright reminds Flynn that two months earlier, he (Tenny) had been the one to authorize the payment of salary for Flynn's four days on suspension. Errol shoots back, "If you think you are doing me a favor giving me that four days' salary, as far as I'm concerned, you can stick it."

When asked one more time to work until six o'clock, Flynn replies, "No, and you can repeat for me, 'I will not work beyond five o'clock on an eight o'clock call at the studio.'"[51] There then follows an extended absence by Flynn, claiming a lung infection, that shuts down production through the end of March. Perhaps these episodes are Flynn's way, consciously or unconsciously, of wresting control from those authority figures attempting to oppress him. Or perhaps he is suffering from a

An artist captures the likenesses of the ownership team of the Pirates' Den nightclub...except Flynn seems conspicuously beastly in the portrait at lower right.

Errol Flynn, Ronald Reagan, and Alan Hale are Allied flyers downed behind enemy lines and hiding out in Goering's railroad car in this scene from *Forced Landing*, which was later retitled *Desperate Journey*. Despite the kinship he felt with Reagan and longtime pal Hale, this was not a happy production for Flynn due to ill health and discontent.

bout of depression induced by his 4-F draft designation. Evidence indicates that he did suffer from incapacitating depression that locked him into Mulholland for days or weeks on end.

Flynn's last love, Beverly Aadland, will tell the British tabloid the *Daily Sketch*, after his death: "He was a complex and introspective man, given to great outbursts of drinking and high living, then reverting suddenly to long, quiet periods of depression and despair." This isn't a tendency Flynn acquires late in life. Depression is his companion all along the way, from childhood. However, there is a distraction in early 1942. A houseguest.

John Barrymore stumbles into Mulholland one night and stays three weeks. The liver of the Great Profile is about to shut down, and his mind is going. He camps in the aqua bedroom upstairs above the garage and, whether out of delirium or contempt for humanity, finds it reasonable to urinate out the window rather than walk into the bathroom located just on the other side of his bed. Flynn complains loudly to Barrymore, and to no avail. With brand new window sills stressed by urine, Flynn is stressed as well, and says, "My work about now was really going to hell," which also may account for some of the call-offs during production of *Forced Landing*.[52]

Living with Barrymore should have been a cautionary experience for Flynn, but apparently he doesn't see—or chooses not to dwell on—the similiaries between himself and a young Barrymore, and where a life of reckless hedonism might lead. Instead he moves on full speed ahead in his self-absorbed world, making pictures that are moneymakers, forcing the studio to endure real and imagined illnesses, known to some as "Flynnanigans." In May Flynn is making a new movie, *Gentleman Jim Corbett* (later shortened to *Gentleman Jim*) and negotiating with Warners for a new nine-picture, seven-year contract that creates Flynn's own paper company, Thomson Productions. The studio

Errol Flynn lights a Lucky Strike in his bachelor's paradise, as his number one status symbol, the Gauguin original, hangs over his shoulder.

has just negotiated such a contract with Bette Davis. In effect, Flynn gets some creative control, but not final authority, in three of the Warner pictures to be made out of nine in the contract. By this time he earns $90,000 per picture, paid out at the rate of $6,000 per week. And he needs every penny of it for life in his new home and on the road.

The new contract is signed in October 1942, a chaotic month in a chaotic year. The German army is near Stalingrad. Rommel and Montgomery are slugging it out in a place called El Alamein. American and Japanese aircraft carriers fight a running battle across vast stretches of the Pacific. In the United States, the war machine kicks into high gear and now stamps out bombers and tanks and rifles and machine guns and bullets.

On Mulholland Drive, Flynn is still dating Mary Ann Hyde, who has been taking dictation on his South Pacific-to-Hollywood adventure novel, *Charlie Bow-Tie*. Hyde has just finished work in the Charles Boyer all-star anthology film, *Flesh and Fantasy*. In fact, she's just landed a photo shoot for *Life* magazine to support the release of the movie. Mary Ann is happy to have a boyfriend of Flynn's caliber, but highly displeased with her boyfriend's roving eye.

This night, Mary Ann isn't around. The October breeze is cool, with the aroma of fresh-cut pine filling the house. Once in a while the sleek frame structure settles with a groan or contracts with a pop and a crack as the sun fades, and on some nights, like this one, these are the only sounds to be heard. Many of Flynn's women report that he is a homebody and ventures out to carouse only on the weekends. And tonight is a weeknight. He has spent the day working on his war picture, *Edge of Darkness*, and now rests in solitude. Until the chime of the doorbell.

Alex approaches Flynn to report that two Los Angeles police detectives want a word, that they are flashing badges and official papers. Flynn meets them in the living room, and it doesn't take a lot of imagination to create long shadows in that endless expanse of glass and pine—a stark black-and-white scene: cops grilling Errol Flynn about his recent activities.

The fearless Flynn starts out glib, but sobers up fast. Sweat would bead on any guy's forehead upon hearing the word *rape* from plainclothes detectives. Flynn can't quite believe it. The cops want to know if he had been preying upon juvenile girls at a party some weeks earlier.

"Do you know a girl named Betty Hansen?" they ask him. He knows lots of girls. Lots and lots of girls. He has preyed upon them; they have preyed upon him. But Betty Hansen—the name doesn't conjure up a face. They ask him to accompany them downtown to Juvenile Hall.

Flynn reaches for the phone and calls his lawyer, Robert Ford. Then he grabs his jacket and hat, steps out the door by the pool and walks with the two cops along the glass dining room doors, around the corner past his garage, to the car parked in the drive beyond, and out into the night.

It's not every day that detectives find themselves in a car with a movie star who has played Robin Hood and General Custer, a matinee idol on intimate terms with the likes of Ann Sheridan and Olivia de Havilland. But how talkative can the actor be? It is one of those life-flashing-before-the-eyes moments, sitting in the cop car, thinking about being a movie star and making all that dough, and the house and yacht and fame and adoration. It's been a good life these past seven years, and will it all go away? Warners is spending millions on his movies, like *Gentleman Jim*, a sure-fire hit ready for release for the Christmas holiday in two months. What the hell will J.L. say when he hears about *this*? The press will grab it and run—columnists Flynn has never met are always willing to take potshots at him. And for what? For no other reason than the fact that he is Errol Flynn, and they are not.

It is a night that starts out like any other at Mulholland Farm, but an hour later, as the car winds down Mulholland toward Cahuenga, it becomes a night that would, for Errol Flynn, never really end at all.

Art imitates life: In mere weeks, Flynn will be shocked to find detectives at the door of Mulholland asking him about statutory rape, but in September 1942, Flynn toils at Warner Brothers in *Edge of Darkness*, his finest dramatic performance of the war years. Here the character portrayed by Ann Sheridan has just been raped by a German soldier, setting off a fight to the finish between villagers and Nazis.

Errol Flynn: Actor

Viewed in retrospect, Errol Flynn could act. Many didn't think so in his day, including such luminaries as Bette Davis, who compared Flynn to the gold standard of the time—Laurence Olivier and Paul Muni—and found him an embarrassment to the silver screen. In retrospect, the M.O. of Olivier and Muni was to deliver stage performances before the unblinking eye of the camera. Flynn learned to play shadings of himself, and remained careful not to stretch beyond his range, taking few chances in the early years.

Said Viveca Lindfors, herself an intense professional and a legendary acting teacher, "He was a brilliant actor. A genius. And didn't know it. He…paid no attention to his talent."[53]

Maureen O'Hara, who co-starred with Flynn in *Against All Flags*, said, "I enjoyed working with Errol because he was a pro. He always came to work prepared. He rehearsed hard and…knew his lines, something I greatly respect in an actor."[54]

Basil Rathbone said of Flynn, "He had talent but how much we shall never know; there were flashes of this talent in all the three pictures we made together."[55]

Flynn began to emerge, not under the direction of the autocratic Michael Curtiz, but with directors he trusted, like Frank Borzage in *Green Light* and William Dieterle in *Another Dawn*. In general, he would work hard for directors he respected. Edmond Goulding drew from Flynn the best performance of his career in *The Dawn Patrol*. Flynn's considerable talent can be viewed in *Elizabeth and Essex*, that pressure-cooker production, when he turned in a credible performance under the direction of his least favorite director, Curtiz, and his least favorite leading lady, Davis, with the eyes of the studio firmly fixed on him.

Flynn's salad days as an actor, such as they were, occurred during the Mulholland years, with Lewis Milestone in *Edge of Darkness* and Raoul Walsh in *They Died With Their Boots On*, *Northern Pursuit*, *Uncertain Glory*, and *Objective, Burma!* Then the malaise set in and lasted for five straight Warner Brothers pictures. He turned in stronger and more sober work for MGM, but by then his opportunities to perform were waning.

Greer Garson felt that if Flynn hadn't died so young, "he would probably have emerged as the serious actor he longed to be."[56] But the truth is that when he made his Hollywood "comeback," playing a series of derelicts in *The Sun Also Rises*, *The Roots of Heaven*, and *Too Much, Too Soon*, his mind and body were shot and he couldn't remember his lines with regularity. His talent was simply gone.

During the span of his career he was self-deprecating about his abilities, but if Errol Flynn didn't believe in Errol Flynn the actor, why did he act like a fan and collect 16mm prints of all of Errol Flynn's movies? And why did he build for himself a wing with a movie theater in it at Mulholland Farm in 1945? In his last interview, a week before his death, he was asked if he watched his old films and he nonchalantly replied, "No, I don't often look at them." His girlfriend, Beverly Aadland, interjected, "Oh yes you do, and I've heard you say, 'My, I used to be good looking in those days!'"[57]

Kirk Douglas started his career at Warner Brothers during the later Flynn years, and summed up Errol Flynn's talent this way: "Some people didn't consider him much of an actor, but I did. I think he had great personal style that you don't see anymore. There are very few actors who could carry off Robin Hood the way he did."[58]

Opposite page: Director Edmond Goulding (in hat) manages to coax from Errol Flynn his best performance of all in *The Dawn Patrol*. Here Flynn shares a tense moment with Basil Rathbone. (John McElwee Collection)

Errol Flynn's mouthpiece, Jerry Giesler, interviews prospective jurors as his client looks on, the soul of youthful innocence, on the first day of the rape trial in Los Angeles Court, January 11, 1943.

lynn will remember it in his memoirs as a long car ride, moving ever farther away from the sanctuary of Mulholland Farm, that he completes in silence. Betty Hansen. Betty Hansen. He cannot for the life of him remember a Betty Hansen.

Tawdry business like this might cause the studio to release him, citing the morals clause in his contract. His standing with the public will certainly suffer. Sure, he's a carouser, a bad boy, but people seem to love him for it. They not only forgive him his escapades, from womanizing to drunken brawls, they revel in them. He stands alone in the hearts of the public. Errol Flynn, swashbuckler. But rape. This, he knows, is different.

Maybe the studio can cover it up. A payoff to the police here, to a reporter there—it happens all the time in Hollywood. With his mind racing, he chain-smokes the miles away.

Here Flynn's life intersects that of 17-year-old Betty Hansen of Nebraska, visiting her sister in Los Angeles. On Saturday, September 26, 1942, Hansen is one of many young cuties at a Bel Air party that Flynn attends on St. Pierre Road at the home of Freddy McEvoy. She is taken there by a Warner Brothers Studio clerk at the invitation of Buster Wiles. A good-looking, blonde nightclub singer named Lynn Boyer also attends, and entertainment is provided by an exotic dancer named Agnes Toupes. Hansen admits later to going there specifically to meet Flynn, after having sought advice on ways to play up to him. It's common knowledge that Flynn likes them young and pretty and never gives a thought to checking a birth certificate.

As if she had written the script herself, Betty not-so-subtly sits on his lap and shares cocktails, and Flynn is inspired to take her upstairs to one of McEvoy's spare bedrooms, and they have sex and make pillow talk about the star helping the farmgirl find work in the movies. Flynn dutifully takes Hansen's address and slips Hansen his unlisted phone number—which becomes a key piece of evidence supporting the seedy girl's claim that she is on intimate terms with the screen star.

Betty Hansen is picked up as a runaway and becomes an ingredient in a perfect storm that will consume Errol Flynn. Graft and corruption are rife in Los Angeles, and stars and studios pay off law enforcement officials to forgive offenses. But Jack Warner has always resisted, so law enforcement will make an example of Warner Brothers by fingering one of its biggest investments, Errol Flynn. The district attorney strongarms underage Betty Hansen into charging Flynn with statutory rape.

The story breaks in mid-October 1942, and newspapers across the country print the rape charge against Flynn. The first accounts are buried deep in the papers, but soon Flynn's exploits will claim above-the-fold, front-page real estate and bump coverage of World War II.

The police question Flynn about the incident. Reporters catch on. Flashbulbs pop. Moviegoers nationwide gasp. *Errol Flynn is a rapist?* Flynn later admits to being shocked by the word. He will say in *My Wicked, Wicked Ways*, "Rape to me meant picking up a chair and hitting some young lady over the head with it and having your wicked way. I hadn't done any of these things."[59]

Errol Flynn Defendant In Rape Charge

Film Star Accused Of Illicit Relations With Stage-Struck Girl, 17.

(Picture on Page 24)

LOS ANGELES, Oct. 17. (AP)— Actor Errol Flynn, who has won many a fair maiden's heart on the silver screen but wasn't able to make a success of his own marriage, today was defendant in a rape charge involving a 17-year-old stage-struck girl, who said he told her he "was very fond ot me and would get me a job."

A complaint, issued on instructions from District Attorney John F. Dockweiler, alleged that on the night of September 27 Flynn raped Betty Hansen of Lincoln, Neb., during a party at the fashionable Bel Air home of Fred McEvoy, wealthy British sportsman and former Olympic bobsled champion.

"He told me he would call me the next night," Juvenile Officer Dorothy Pulas quoted the girl as saying. "I waited for three nights, but he never called."

Under $1,000 Bail

Father of a 17-month-old son, Flynn, who was divorced last April by Screen Actress Lily Damita, was released under $1,000 bail pending preliminary hearing October 23.

"I can't understand what all this is about," said the 33-year-old British-born actor in denying the charge. "I hardly spoke to the girl, and certainly I did not harm her."

The complaint against Flynn was signed by Mrs. Jack Marsden, a sister, with whom Miss Hansen lived. It also charged three youthful film studio employes with making subsequent morals attacks upon the girl.

Listed as Armand Knapp, 18; Morrie Black, 22, and Joseph Geraldi, 20, they already are in custody.

Under California law, a sex offense against a girl under 18, regardless of consent, constitutes rape.

Left: Newspapers across America at first gave the Flynn story just a little play, as with this page ten account in the Fort Wayne *News-Sentinel*. Before long Flynn would push his way onto page one, above the fold, and steal headlines from the World War. Above: Three grim figures appear in Los Angeles Court for the preliminary hearing: attorney Robert Ford, accused rapist Errol Flynn, and famed defense counselor Jerry Giesler.

The case goes to a grand jury, and a dazed Flynn finds himself amidst a spectacle. "Crowds swarmed the courthouse," he says. "The people were strung out in front of the place, and I wanted to shrink to the ground with shame." America now knows that Errol Flynn is a wolf, both on-screen and off.

"Women banged on the doors of Mulholland House like ice drops in a hailstorm," he says. The grand jury convenes, hears the case, and promptly throws it out. In October 1942 Flynn returns to Mulholland with McEvoy and celebrates.[60]

Two days later, the district attorney proceeds with the case against Errol Flynn. The D.A. finds a record of another underage girl who claims Flynn seduced her at age 15.

Her name is Peggy LaRue Satterlee, a dancer at the Florentine Gardens. She had accompanied Flynn aboard his yacht the first weekend of August 1941 for a spear fishing trip photographed by Peter Stackpole, who had also taken the photos for Flynn's famous 1938 cover and inside story spread in *Life* magazine.

Had Flynn been intimate with Satterlee, a worldly knockout of a showgirl with a shady past? Buster Wiles will claim that Flynn had been suffering from sinus trouble on the Stackpole weekend and checked into a hospital soon thereafter. But taking one look at Satterlee clears the matter right on up—a luscious and willing brunette in a swimsuit on a quiet, weekend cruise to Catalina with Errol Flynn. There had been others aboard, but Flynn had lots of motive and plenty of opportunity.

There are hijinx aplenty in this case, not only by notorious wolf Errol Flynn but by the Los Angeles district attorney, who is playing for high political and cash stakes. The message being sent loud and clear to all of Hollywood through Jack Warner: You will pay for protection and you will like it, or we will nail your stars.

Flynn is again dragged away from Mulholland. This time he is placed in a holding cell. Flynn's hard-drinking young attorney, Robert Ford, makes an emergency call to the number-one defense attorney in the nation, Harold Lee "Jerry" Giesler.

At 56, Giesler possesses a gentle round face and presents himself as a father figure. In the courtroom he is a tiger, having earned his spurs in defending Otto Sanhuber in the strange, "Love in the Loft" case, in which Sanhuber remained hidden in an attic for years to tend to a philandering wife—until the attic dweller was spotted by the husband, whom Sanhuber shot and killed. The defense team, including Giesler, got the defendant off with a lesser manslaughter conviction. Giesler also had defended L.A.

theater mogul Alexander Pantages against a charge of indecent sexual assault against a 17-year-old girl in two trials, in 1930 and 1931. "If a single client can be said to have made a lawyer," said Giesler, "Pantages made me."[61]

The case gives Giesler important expertise in defending a man charged with raping an underage girl—the jury's sympathy tends to favor the girl and not the man. He also learns how to gather evidence, play the press, and battle the office of the Los Angeles District Attorney.

Giesler finds the claimant in the Pantages case, young Eunice Pringle, to be a "remarkably lush seventeen," and Pantages "a scrawny little man." When Pringle appears in court, she hides her curves in a schoolgirl outfit, her hair in pigtails. By the end of the day it's even worse for the

Errol Flynn's two accusers, 16-year-old exotic dancer Peggy Larue Satterlee (left) and 17-year-old former Nebraskan Betty Hansen meet for the first time as Flynn's trial begins on January 11, 1943, in a Los Angeles courtroom.

The starstruck nine women and three men of the Errol Flynn jury, with a tenth woman (top right) serving as alternate. Mrs. Ruby Anderson (bottom left) was the foreman who would read the verdict on all three counts to a terrified Errol Flynn three weeks—and many twists and turns—after this photograph was taken.

defense team as headlines scream, STORY SOBBED BY PRINGLE GIRL.

Giesler then starts to work. He asks the judge to require the plaintiff to appear in court in the outfit she was wearing when "attacked." The judge agrees, and in slinks a different Eunice Pringle in a red dress "cut low enough to display quite a lot of her," said Giesler, "and when she swung her hips up onto the stand she undulated." Giesler's examination centers on Pringle's sexual past, and the judge stops him. Pantages is sentenced to 50 years in state prison.[62]

But the tireless Giesler files a brilliant appeal and earns a second trial in 1931. This time around, Giesler uncovers the true motive of Pringle and an accomplice to get Pantages to book their act in his theatre—or else. The verdict the second time around: not guilty.

If ever Errol Flynn should thank anyone, it's Eunice Pringle for her ill-conceived plot against Alexander Pantages, which had served to forge in silver one formidable knight of the courtroom—soft-spoken Jerry Giesler.

Eleven years later, when Robert Ford puts out a call to the "magnificent mouthpiece," Giesler, the veteran sees in an instant that Flynn has "the dice of public opinion loaded against him."[63] On November 23, 1942, Giesler stands with Flynn and Ford at a preliminary hearing in Los Angeles Court before Municipal Judge Byron J. Walters. Hansen and Satterlee testify, and Judge Walters holds Flynn for trial on three counts of statutory rape. He is arraigned, officially charged, and fingerprinted. Reporter Florabel Muir, who knows and has written about Flynn, watches the proceeding and says, "If Errol was panicky, he managed to conceal it. He was courteous and dreadfully serious."[64]

The real story behind the Errol Flynn rape extravaganza of 1943 seems to be this: young upstart John Dockweiler runs against incumbent L.A. District Attorney Buron Fitts and beats him. Fitts has "working relationships" with the studios, including Warner Brothers. J.L. refuses to support Dockweiler, who vows to get even. And down goes Flynn.

For the record, Dockweiler says of his decision to try Flynn, "I must let the public know that all men and women are equal when they come before our courts and that no one can violate the law and escape punishment because of wealth or position."[65]

The trial begins on January 11, 1943, in Los Angeles County Superior Court. Judge Leslie E. Still presides. Every

If only America had known what was going on at Mulholland while Flynn was fighting for his freedom. He was secretly playing host to a young girl, Blanca Rosa Welter, whom he had met in Mexico City, November 13, 1942, on her 19th birthday. At that time he had fled the States to gather his wits after being held over for trial on statutory rape charges.

Welter was born in Mexico but grew up in Europe and the Middle East and fled the Holy Land just ahead of the Nazis. Unlike many of the girls orbiting Flynn, this one was well traveled and sharp minded. Her beauty eclipsed even Damita's, and Blanca could carry on a conversation about something other than clothes and shoes—and in several languages. In her 1962 autobiography she recounted the night Flynn claimed her virginity and then described his emotional distance afterward.[66] For Flynn it was the end of the chase.

Errol signed Blanca to a six-month personal contract and shipped her to Mulholland, where she remained during the rape trial. He reported that while Blanca was a kept woman, she had her teeth capped and charged it to him, along with a new wardrobe and hairstyle. Flynn junked her unattractive name, changing it to Linda Christian in reference to Fletcher Christian of Bounty fame, and arranged a screen test under the direction of Raoul Walsh at Warner Brothers, with Flynn feeding her lines. Errol Flynn taught Linda Christian about nightlife on the Sunset Strip and introduced her to such luminaries as Sam Goldwyn and Earl Carroll.

In the last days of the trial, Jerry Giesler told Buster Wiles to "disappear" so that he couldn't be subpoenaed to testify.[67] The reason had nothing to do with the fact that Buster had participated in the weekend cruise with Peggy Satterlee. Rather, Buster was living at Mulholland during the trial and might have blown Flynn's credibility at the last minute by answering questions about a certain young houseguest at the Farm.

At the conclusion of the rape trial, Linda left Mulholland to begin clawing her way up the ladder in Hollywood. She achieved notoriety first as a Goldwyn Girl, then as a B-movie actress, the wife of Tyrone Power, and finally a globe-trotting playgirl. She posed nude on a sun-drenched Mexican beach for Diego Rivera and found herself dubbed "Headline Huntress" by Elsa Maxwell. Linda Christian is one of the last remaining luminaries who knew Flynn and Mulholland in their heyday—in this case, during the darkest days of Flynn's life.

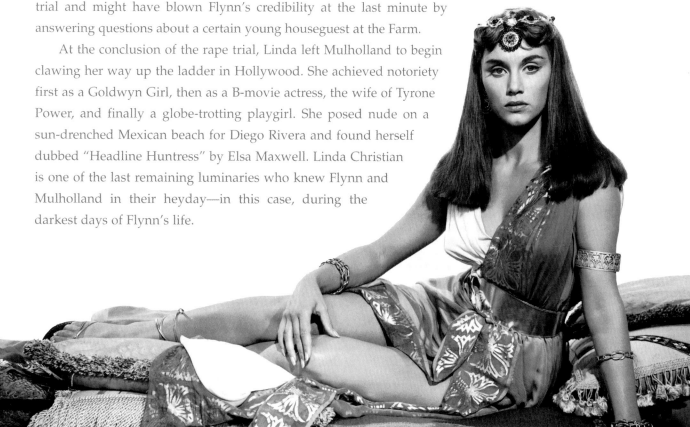

On January 28, 1943, Assistant District Attorney John Hopkins pointed out testimony from the preliminary hearing to Errol Flynn as he sat on the stand for cross-examination during the rape trial. "Flynn was a good witness," said defense attorney Jerry Giesler in something of an understatement.

morning Flynn prepares himself at Mulholland and then rides downtown, most often with Buster Wiles. A jury is selected; Giesler would recall with satisfaction, "I managed to get nine women on the jury, believing that they would be more kindly disposed than men toward the boyishly handsome screen actor."[68]

Betty Hansen takes the stand first and quickly proves to be no Olivia de Havilland; she's an ordinary-looking, uneducated Nebraska farmgirl who seems far out of place in a Los Angeles courtroom. Deputy D.A. Thomas Cochran guides her through testimony about the day, four months earlier, when she had met Flynn at the party in Freddy McEvoy's Bel Air mansion. She had shared drinks with him...sat on his lap...allowed him to lead her upstairs and

remove her clothes in a McEvoy guest bedroom...and have sex with her, leaving his shoes and socks on. It is the first of many private details aired in open court that whittles away his soul.

On cross-examination, Giesler draws out her motive for seeking to attend the McEvoy party: She had heard Flynn would be there and played up to him, and even decided she would have sex with him, in the hope he would get her work in the movies. She reports that the lovemaking lasts an impressive 50 minutes, and that Flynn had been complimentary of her breasts and "fanny."

The case takes a bizarre turn when Lynn Boyer, another guest at McEvoy's party, appearing under subpoena by the D.A., bursts into tears and threatens to jump out the

Gaunt, pale, and lacking sleep, a crestfallen Errol Flynn, no longer quite so fearless, reads lurid details of his sex life on page one of the Los Angeles *Daily Sentinel* during a break in his three-week trial for statutory rape.

Above: At the preliminary hearing, a cool, calm, and collected Lynn Boyer chatted with the dreamy defendant. Boyer was a lounge singer who had been invited to the McEvoy party where Flynn met Hansen. Below: At the trial, Boyer threatened to jump out the window rather than testify against Flynn.

window of the courtroom rather than testify against heart-throb Errol Flynn.

As the days grind by, and the routine repeats—trial by day, Mulholland by night—Flynn grows pale and gaunt. But he doesn't crack in public under conditions that are described in a United Press story dated January 25, 1943: "The bailiff, hopeful of giving all comers a chance to see the wavy-haired Flynn in the flesh, has evolved a system of keeping all spectators in line, as at a movie box office, and emptying the courtroom four times a day.

"At each recess Flynn, who has managed for the most part to remain debonair even when the testimony was at its most embarrassing, has been mobbed by his fans. They have demanded autographs, torn buttons off his clothes, and struggled for the privilege of touching him."

Hardened beat reporters witness the goings on, day in and day out. Many have spent time with Flynn at the studio or at Mulholland while stringing for the fan magazines. Many hadn't cared for his conceited air and changeable moods, but now they see the bad boy in a new light.

"Even the ladies of the press fell for Flynn," reporter Muir will say in her memoirs. "Hard-boiled reporters like Peggy Cook, who has covered the district attorney's beat for many years, and Agnes Underwood, now the city editor of the Los Angeles *Herald-Express*, came under the spell of his charm."[69]

After the Hansen matter has been thoroughly investigated by the D.A., Peggy Satterlee takes the stand, and electricity snaps in the air. Satterlee is a knockout of a girl and an articulate witness. She had gone sailing with Flynn,

Wiles, *Life* photographer Peter Stackpole, and some others on *Sirocco* to Catalina Island and back. The cruise would serve as a backdrop for a Stackpole photo shoot, and Satterlee was to be set dressing. She testifies that early Sunday morning, August 3, 1941, Flynn entered her room as she lay in bed. "Why do you have to bother a nice girl?" she says she told him and claims he responded, "I wanted to be nice to you, but you asked for it so you will get it."

After a day of photographs and spearfishing, she states, the *Sirocco* was returning to port when Flynn led her below deck because she wanted to look at the moon, and Flynn said it looked better through a porthole. She reports that below he "said, since he had possession of me once, naturally why wouldn't I let him do it this time." There then occurred, she testifies, another act of forcible rape.[70]

Defense attorney Jerry Giesler strikes a pose that recreates his summation for the jury during the last day of Flynn's rape trial. The defendant has endured three weeks of proceedings and now awaits his fate, which will soon be in the hands of the jury.

Flynn provides for attorney Robert Ford a sketch of *Sirocco*, the yacht on which sexual activities with 15-year-old Peggy Satterlee took place in 1941.

Blanca Welter (later Linda Christian), Flynn's house-guest at the time, wanders into the dining room one evening to find that, "Errol was shouting from the head of the table, 'I don't care, I tell you, if it takes every cent I've got—I'm going to throw this thing back in their faces.' Five other men at the table murmured in agreement, and Errol introduced them as 'just a few of my varied acquaintances.'" Welter reports that this group, which includes Jerry Giesler, Robert Ford, and members of their investigative team, along with Flynn confederates Wiles and Freddy McEvoy, huddle often at Mulholland during the trial as Flynn's drinking picks up noticeably.[71]

A week into the proceedings, the prosecution learns that two of the jurors had expressed opinions about Flynn's guilt or innocence before they had been seated. All the attorneys and Flynn rush into Judge Still's chambers—the D.A. asking for a mistrial and Giesler asserting that if a mistrial is granted, Flynn would be put into a situation of double jeopardy if he were to be tried again.

Flynn quips, "I don't mind rooters in the jury box, but they ought to keep their mouths shut."

Judge Still orders the trial to continue, and Giesler goes on the attack. He goes before the press and says, "We are seeking no compromise. We are denying the charges right down the line."[72]

As if scripted by Hollywood, Giesler ambles along, all the while establishing the credibility of his client and the unreliability of the claimants. He makes the jury aware that

Hansen has been charged with some "unusual" underage sex crimes and is seeking to avoid a stint in Juvenile Hall by agreeing to make the charge against Flynn.

Giesler really goes to work on the character of Peggy Larue Satterlee. He alludes to a photo of Satterlee posing semi-nude, but doesn't show the jury. He just gives a tsk-tsk wag of his head. Then he destroys Peggy's credibility in claiming she had actually seen the moon through the port-hole that night—it would have been positioned on the opposite side of the boat from her room below decks as *Sirocco* returned from Catalina. He draws a map of the heavens on a chalkboard and begins his dissertation, "*This* is Sirius." One of the women jurors murmurs, "It certainly is." Giesler infers that for the claimant to have even glimpsed the moon, she must have X-ray vision.

Upon taking the stand in his own defense, Flynn makes a solid witness. "He was good because he answered forthright-ly everything asked of him," said Giesler. "He didn't change his pace between direct examination and his cross-examination."

Flynn's answers to the ques-tions posed by the prosecution, according to Giesler, "were enough to make any sane man wonder if he and Miss Satterlee were talking about the same voy-age on the same boat, or even whether it had traversed the same body of water."[73] Flynn denies having any sort of interest in, or erotic contact with, either Peggy Satterlee or Betty Hansen.

Giesler maneuvers the District Attorney into calling a Canadian Air Force pilot to the witness stand—a man 28 years

Peggy's senior—and makes it part of the public record that Satterlee and the pilot had made a late-night visit to an L.A. mortuary and that young Peggy had cavorted in sexual fashion among the corpses. Giesler also reveals that Satterlee had been an exotic dancer and had had an abor-tion (a felony in itself at that time)—all by age 16.

On the other hand, Giesler has to tapdance around Errol Flynn's pet names for Satterlee—"J.B." and "S.Q.Q." In other words, Flynn knew his date was young enough to be jailbait or the equally euphemistic San Quentin Quail.

Buster Wiles (left) waits with a nervous Errol Flynn during the 12-hour jury deliberation that will decide his fate on three counts of statutory rape.

Buster Wiles claims that in the latter stages of the trial, Giesler asks, "Buster, can you disappear?"[74] It seems that Giesler, who has seen Rosa Welter at Mulholland, fears the information will go public, and Wiles, a houseguest at the Farm, could be called by the prosecution and ruin an otherwise strong presentation by the defense.

Flynn's recklessness, his penchant for young female flesh, is affirmed by Joan Leslie, a winsome underage Warner Brothers starlet at the time of the trial. "Mr. Flynn had quite a reputation," says Leslie, "so I was kept as *farrrr* away as possible—but I wanted to meet him. I remember one time at a party, when he was in legal trouble, he just walked over to me and said, 'I thought I'd say hello. I'm Errol Flynn.' I said, 'Oh, I'm so glad to meet you!' What a lot of charm that man had! A flash went off, and in no time publicity men separated us, and took the film, and said, 'No more pictures!' I was whisked away. And *that* was my introduction to Errol Flynn."[75]

After three sensational weeks, closing arguments in the Flynn trial are heard from Deputy D.A. Cochran and Giesler, who reminds the jury of the checkered past of both accusers, and that the whole case smells like a "fix." Judge Still charges the jury on February 6, 1943, advising the group of the abortion and the other factors: "If you believe Miss Satterlee is guilty of such an act, then you have the right to take into consideration her state of mind while she was testifying in this court. Also, if you believe that Miss Hansen engaged in an illegal act with a man, you may con-

"Not guilty." Assistant D.A. Thomas Cochran sits dejectedly on the banister as Errol Flynn goes down the line and shakes hands with each of the 12 giddy jurors after they exonerate him on February 7, 1943. Here he presses flesh with foreman Ruby Anderson.

sider the effect upon her mind and her statements. You may consider that both girls were hoping for leniency."

Judge Still goes further and brings up the issue of the birth certificates of the two girls in question. "A birth certificate is not conclusive. It is only prima-facie evidence. If you entertain a reasonable doubt in your mind as to the ages of the witnesses, you should give the defendant the benefit of the doubt."

The jury takes what Giesler calls "an interminable time" in deliberation. Flynn paces, plays solitaire, smokes a pack of Luckies, and chats with Wiles—now back from his sudden "vacation." Says Wiles, "I kept telling the kid he couldn't lose, but the last few hours he got to chewing his nails."[76] It is here, after 33 carefree years, that the fearless Flynn finally makes his last stand.

The jury takes 12 hours to deliberate and returns the next day. Flynn, Ford, and Giesler stand, faces ashen. No one breathes in the courtroom. The jury foreman, Ruby Anderson, reads the verdicts on all three counts: not guilty.

Judge Still tells the jury, "The evidence was sufficient for you to have arrived at a verdict in either direction. Under the circumstances I think you have arrived at a proper verdict."

Flynn leaps across the desk to the jury box, flings a leg over the wood railing, and shakes the hands of each juror.

Satterlee's reaction is heard by courtroom reporters: "I hate him more than anyone else in the world. I think it's horrible. I knew those women on the jury would acquit him. They sat there and looked at him adoringly just like he was their son or something." She slumps and says finally, "I wish those police had left me out of this altogether."

One of the jurors, Mrs. Nellie S. Minear, says, "We knew Flynn was not guilty a long time ago, but we didn't want to come out too soon because we wondered what the public might think."

When told of this, Flynn thinks of his long, tortured hours of waiting. "That's a fine thing," he gripes. "I think I aged ten years while they were fiddling around worrying about public opinion. I didn't know jurors had to care." On the other hand, he has spent a month making sure they *did* care by playing the boyish, sober, and serious craftsman— a guy it was impossible not to like.

Then he says, "I know that an innocent man armed only with the knowledge of innocence isn't always sure of getting justice. I appreciate, now that it is all over, what a dangerous spot I was in." His ace in the hole? By his own admission in *My Wicked, Wicked Ways*, he had arranged for a plane to be standing ready to fly him straight to Mexico if, at any point, it looked like curtains.

In the press room at the Hall of Justice, Flynn says to the reporters, "I'm sure going to miss all you interesting people."[77]

To acknowledge what he considers to be favorable coverage, Flynn, Ford, and Wiles show up at a farewell party thrown by the press at Agnes Underwood's home two days later. They are armed with a case of booze. It will be his last friendly gesture to reporters for a long time; he will turn on them, because he believes they turned on him.

That evening, members of the press try Flynn in a kangaroo court to the amusement of everyone but Robert Ford, who frowns on such a mockery of the judicial process. In the end Flynn is convicted and sentenced to life...on board *Sirocco*, in the custody of a dozen 18-year-old girls.

Flynn drinks a lot and has a blast, thinking the rape trial is behind him. He doesn't realize it, but even as newspapers emblazon the verdict across page one in headline type, and newsreels flash images of the courtroom on silver screens across America, a stake has been driven through the heart of fearless, carefree, fun-loving Errol Flynn of 7740 Mulholland Highway in Hollywood.

Soon after the rape trial, Flynn poses for still photographs at Warner Brothers, his face revealing the full impact of the courtroom ordeal and its aftermath. He has learned that he is infamous and that the phrase "in like Flynn" has entered the American lexicon—at his expense.

Errol Flynn doesn't know at once that Hollywood has scorned him—not until he returns to Mulholland and throws a party. "I thought I ought to start living again, seeing people, find out who my friends were," he will recall in *My Wicked, Wicked Ways*. "Mulholland House was loaded with flowers, liquor, lights. I invited just about everybody in the community to come to my house for an evening of fun.... Along about the middle of the evening I realized practically nobody was coming."[78] Reports Buster Wiles, "It was a dismal flop."[79]

In mid-February 1943 Errol Flynn learns where an accused rapist, acquitted or not, stands in Hollywood. He begins to understand that one doesn't celebrate the beating of a rape charge. One endures it. An awful feeling settles in, as he puts it all together, from his role as a pawn between J.L. Warner and Los Angeles City Hall to his squandering of a productive career through participation in a series of meaningless dalliances.

His recently completed *Edge of Darkness*, having commenced production prior to the rape charge and wrapped before the start of the trial, will be released in two months and contains a powerhouse lineup of Hollywood talent under the direction of Lewis Milestone, including Ann Sheridan, Walter Huston, Judith Anderson, Ruth Gordon, and a cast of hundreds. On the other hand, his next picture, *Northern Pursuit*, is a grim adventure to be set in the frigid Canadian north, with Raoul Walsh directing on a shoestring. Flynn's co-star will not be a glamour girl like Olivia de Havilland; instead he gets poor Julie Bishop, a competent but faded 1930s actress struggling in an attempted

comeback. It's not just Flynn who's suffering. The entire studio is nearly dark at the moment. A February 22, 1943 wire from J.L. to the New York office advises:

THERE'S NOTHING SHOOTING AT STUDIO NOW THIS FIRST TIME IN 15 YEARS THAT STUDIO IS DARK NEXT WEEK WE START TWO PICTURES ONE STARTING DOUBTFUL JUST CANNOT GET PEOPLE TO WORK ACCOUNT SALARY CEILING HYSTERIA IN EVERYONE'S MIND ACCOUNT WORLD CONDITIONS ETCETERA[80]

Jack Warner sits in his office in Burbank and, within the cauldron of world war, ponders problems great and small. And among his headaches is the Warners bad boy, Errol Flynn, who is now missing work because he claims the fake snow used inside the soundstage on *Northern Pursuit* has infected his lungs. What the hell do you do with a tarnished hypochondriac movie star under contract to your studio for seven long, bitter, and potentially unprofitable years? "Errol was a little boy we had midwifed into the motion picture world," says J.L., "and we had changed his diapers and gotten him his first long pants. We also had millions of dollars tied up in finished pictures, to say nothing of films still to be shot."[81]

Oh, and one more problem J.L. has to consider: Flynn refuses to talk to the press or cooperate in any way with his own studio's PR department.

The studio must devise a long-term strategy to save its multi-million-dollar investment. The solution they decide upon is to reinvent Errol Flynn by crafting a new, serious, introspective persona, focusing not on movies, not on charity work, not on the war. The spotlight of a major campaign to save Errol Flynn's image will shine on a place untouched by the rape scandal: Mulholland Farm.

In late February 1943, Warners photographer Bert Six, camera assistants, a lighting team, a wardrobe specialist, and a makeup artist congregate at Mulholland Farm to photograph Errol Flynn at home.[82] It is an elaborate, immaculately lit, multiple-day shoot in black and white and Kodachrome. Bert Six shoots wide on the house, with Flynn seated by the pool. Six poses Flynn sitting on his diving board, and playing with his Doberman, and tending his animals, and walking the property. They move inside. Flynn, looking pensive or revealing a hint of a smile, is shown in almost every room (except the bedroom). He dresses in a sport jacket and slacks in some photos. In oth-

ers he is clothed casually in a button-down navy shirt, gray pleated slacks, and brown slip-on loafers. At no time does Flynn pose with women. There are no "cut up" or "gag" shots. He is seen in the living room in formal and casual portraits, with wardrobe changes. He poses in front of his Gauguin and his Van Gogh and fiddles with the radio-phonograph under his Manet, and he leans on the mantel beside the moody Decker portrait. He is photographed in front of the bar (but definitely not behind it), and then seated at the desk in his den, deep in thought, and in his easy chair with a book open in his lap and a dog at his feet. Framed images—a Stackpole photo of Flynn taken in the rigging of *Sirocco* from the 1938 *Life* magazine shoot and an inscribed portrait of FDR—sit behind him on the low knotty pine shelves.

Flynn poses beside his Van Gogh, popularly known as *The Man at Sea*, during the Bert Six photo shoot of February 1943.

Then Six photographs the entire house, upstairs and down, from nearly every corner, without Flynn in view.

The Six photos show that time seems to be healing the wounds. Flynn has endured the rape tag, although a new phrase enters the American lexicon that translates to scoring with a girl—in like Flynn. Warner Brothers releases *Northern Pursuit* and then the all-star *Thank Your Lucky Stars*. Bert Six's photos of Flynn at Mulholland are used in publicity for *Lucky Stars* and show America a side of the bad boy they haven't seen.

Flynn begins to allow a few interviews, but only if he approves of the writers. A July 1944 article in *Screen Stars* magazine entitled "Master of Mulholland Farm" takes readers on a photographic tour of the house as seen through the Bert Six lens. The August 1944 issue of *Movieland* includes four more captioned Bert Six photos in an article called, "Is It Fate With Flynn?"

Flynn takes part in a much-publicized and highly successful celebrity tour of U.S. military installations in the

In his living room, Flynn lounges on the table by the window. As noted in the studio caption, the chintz draperies are of green and cream.

Aleutians. He invests in Mulholland parties, like the one in July 1944 that welcomes drinking buddy Bruce Cabot back from military service. This is Mulholland as it has never been—the place he envisioned before the trial. Cabot's party becomes a prestigious three-mogul triumph that includes not only Jack and Ann Warner and Darryl and Virginia Zanuck, but David O. Selznick along with Mary Pickford and Buddy Rogers, newlyweds Burgess Meredith and Paulette Goddard, Elsa Maxwell, Kay Francis, and dozens of others. They dine on suckling pig and ice cream, dance under the stars, and enjoy a show in the pool by professional swimmers and divers. It is one of the most memorable Hollywood parties of the war years as well as Flynn's triumphant return to grace.

But his restless soul courts danger at every turn. Here on this glorious summer day he goes public with his new love, Nora Eddington, a cigarette girl (now 19—18 when he met her) who had been working at the Hall of Justice during the trial. Guests eye Flynn's new paramour suspiciously—she's a good-looking redhead riding the edge of plump, and she's *very* young. Fourteen years younger than Flynn, in fact. What the guests at the party don't know is that she is also three months pregnant in what could become, if Flynn isn't careful, another messy scandal that might confirm his attraction to teenaged girls and validate the claims of accusers Hansen and Satterlee. But the whispers remain whispers, and the party becomes another verse in the ballad of Errol Flynn.

Flynn's association with Nora Eddington, toxic from its inception, reflects the dark night into which he is passing. "I would never be a boon to any woman dreaming of domestic bliss," he will say later. "I had, after all, met Nora during the rape trial and agreeably married her shortly thereafter. There was little in the situation to make me inwardly convivial to our marriage."[83]

Flynn seems intent on sabotaging his life as fast as Warner Brothers is trying to save it. The studio has supported this new focus on Mulholland and also Flynn's participation in the USO tour of the Aleutians and a bond tour to New Orleans. At the studio he invests his talent into an anti-heroic character, Jean Picard, in the Raoul Walsh picture, *Uncertain Glory*. It is the first film released as a Thomson Production, with Flynn the producer. In retrospect it shows Flynn the actor at his finest, underplaying a difficult role, salting it with his own ambiguous personality. The film receives a cool reception. His next picture is the rugged World War II adventure, *Objective, Burma!* Here he

When Nora Eddington first hit the Hollywood scene in 1943, Flynn's friends told her that she had a face for motion pictures. But Nora settled on being Mrs. Errol Flynn and made just one appearance in a film—the closing scene of *Adventures of Don Juan*, released just two months before their divorce was announced.

spends weeks on location, loses weight, goes down with a recurrence of malaria, and watches as the film is blindsided by pans upon its February 1945 release. The story of American paratroopers raiding a Japanese base is a tense reworking of the 1940 *Northwest Passage*. Reviews in the U.S. press are excellent; but the British press and military scream bloody murder. Lord Louis Mountbatten calls a press conference and denounces *Objective, Burma!* as "a loathsome American production that degrades the British."[84] The criticism has nothing to do with Flynn's work—the British are offended because it is *they* who have fought the Japanese in Burma, not the Americans. But for Flynn it is another contaminated enterprise.

Flynn's picture after *Objective, Burma!* is *San Antonio*, a Texas western, and Flynn hates to make westerns. But there are also "inside" touches, as when a beautiful senorita is suprised by Flynn and his friend while taking a bath and flees screaming. "Don't run away, honey!" he calls, flashing his grin and leering. "We won't look!"

As early as May 1944, during production of *Burma*, a new project is discussed, a picture for Flynn about the legendary lover, Don Juan. It will be Robin Hood Hits Adolescence, with Flynn buckling swashes while giving a nod to his offscreen exploits as a very naughty ladies man. It's also a way for the studio to use its troublesome leading man to best business advantage; J.L. loves the idea!

Perhaps because studio executives are so high on the idea, Flynn balks. Flynn often balks, studio papers reveal, and jumps at every chance to make the Powers That Be squirm. Director Robert Florey is assigned to the project. Flynn decides he doesn't want Florey. But fate intervenes in the form of Lili Damita, who wants to haul Flynn into court for failing to meet his alimony payments. She hears all this talk of her ex-husband's extravagant parties, blockbuster films, and new production company—the same guy who can't write a monthly alimony check.

On November 28, 1944, a memo to Jack Warner reads: "Errol Flynn will probably be hauled to court on the Damita case—he has renewed his request now to pick up a couple of weeks' salary to make settlement and avoid the embarrassment and publicity that will ensue. Do you want to reconsider in light of his agreeing to be a good boy on DON JUAN and accept Florey?"

The day after Christmas, J.L. receives another memo, this one from producer Jerry Wald:

"Dear J. L.: For your information, on Saturday I sent as requested by Errol Flynn, a final script on DON JUAN to his house, by special messenger."[85]

Flynn is directed to report on January 11, 1945, for makeup and wardrobe tests. But soon thereafter, he takes a powder and heads out of town. On February 4, J.L. cables Flynn in care of Freddy McEvoy in New York City, demanding that he return to work. The next several weeks involve a cat-and-mouse game with Flynn avoiding the project, one day claiming dental problems and the very next, "undulant fever." Then a strike hits Hollywood and shuts down production at Warners into 1946. The project involving Flynn as Don Juan is shelved. Only a few wardrobe and makeup stills remain to give a hint of how Flynn might have played Don Juan while he was still in something resembling his prime.

At a December 29, 1945, party hosted by David Selznick, a drunk Errol Flynn makes an unkind remark to John Huston, who is dating Olivia de Havilland. Huston's demand that they "step outside" begins one of the classic brawls in Hollywood history and leaves Flynn the victor and both men broken and bloodied. Olivia has left Flynn behind and is in love with John Huston, and booze seems to bring Flynn's resentment, or insecurity, or remorse, to the surface. Olivia says later, "I don't know what the remark was, but Errol might have tried to provoke John."[86]

"Errol must have been spoiling for trouble," says Huston in his memoirs, and Selznick is furious that the inci-

A 35-year-old Errol Flynn poses in early *Don Juan* publicity photos taken in January 1945, as the picture was due to commence production. A series of circumstances will lead to a two-and-a-half-year delay in shooting. By the time Errol Flynn made *Adventures of Don Juan* from October 1947 to April 1948, he was an alcohol- and drug-addicted shell of his former vibrant self. One can only wonder how a younger Flynn would have fared in portraying the legendary lover.

dent has wrecked his party. The back-and-forth nighttime brawl is well documented, sending both men to the hospital. The next day, according to Huston, a now-sober Flynn calls to see how he's doing.[87] The fight is but one of dozens of pugilistic endeavors in which mean-drunk Flynn participated. He wins most, including the Huston bout, by decision but loses some as well, depending on the opponent and level of intoxication. Under the headline, "Actor Flynn Down for Short Count in 'One-Punch' Fight," a newspaper article from the previous year tells of an encounter at Sonja Henie's birthday party. Late in the evening, after most guests have departed, Flynn says the wrong thing to Henie in front of her husband, Marine Captain Dan Topping, one of Errol's tennis pals. "I guess he hit me and I went down," says a sheepish and sober Flynn the next day.[88]

Clark Gable will get to know Flynn in the late 1940s and calls him "a colorful bastard, tough as nails."[89]

It would be nice but inaccurate to see Errol Flynn as Mel Brooks will choose to memorialize him in *My Favorite Year*, as a lovable, sanguine, self-aware, funny drunk. But that isn't Flynn. If the surface were to be scraped off the Brooks character, Alan Swann, sweet, remorseful sadness would ooze out. Scratch the veneer on Errol Flynn, and anger bubbles underneath. At Mother and Lili, at the D.A., at Betty and Peggy, at the press, at J.L., and at Nora.

His life is a shambles, with the Flynn-Eddington marriage hitting the rocks early and often. He rings in the new year of 1946 by painting the town with Ida Lupino, a woman he openly and completely adores. Nora does her own carousing with actor Robert Hutton.[90]

The Flynn-Lupino relationship is deep and interesting, and of all Flynn's women, it is "Ides," or "Lupe"—his two pet names for her—who comes closest to being his idea of a baroness for Mulholland. Ida says of Flynn: "He'd call and say, 'Lupe, come over here. There's a daughter and her mother and a deputy here, come help!' And I'd go up and throw them out." She adds, "Can you imagine him having to rape anyone?"[91]

Lupino and Flynn have grown up together at Warner Brothers and finally get the opportunity to work together in the melodrama, *Escape Me Never*. By now Flynn is smitten, but his life is complicated enough already—the last thing he needs on top of a teenaged bride and a baby is a scandalous relationship with one of his co-stars. It seems likely that Flynn cares so much about his Ides that the last thing he wants to do is ruin her life by imposing Errol Flynn on her.

And then there is Flynn's second novel, *Charlie Bow-Tie Comes to America*, retitled by the publisher, *Showdown*, which he had been writing in late-night sessions at Mulholland since the varnish was barely dry in the den. When the book is released early in 1946, critics hate the purple prose and the gritty South Seas plot. *Time* magazine says it features "lusts, busts, tropic moons and cheesecake." During interviews arranged by the publisher, Flynn says he is toying with the idea of acting less and writing more. But the critics scuttle this plan, and although the Flynn name sells great quantities of *Showdown* in hardcover and paperback, he considers the effort a failure. It will take him five years to contemplate another novel, and he will never get to writing it.

Instead, he turns on himself, as revealed in his autobiography: "You are an imposter, Flynn," he remembers thinking. "In real life you don't do any of the things you do on the screen." A

One of the world's archvillains is put to death, and the Thousand Year Reich is crumbling, but, *Good Heavens! Flynn was in a brawl!* This one occurred after Topping KOed Flynn and before the Huston 12 rounder. (Jack Marino Collection)

The once flawless face is now held together with makeup as thick as mortician's wax to hide dissipation, yet sadness permeates in this Warner Brothers portrait. The trial, booze and drugs, fistfights, the humiliation of a 4-F classification, and various ailments were adding up.

He wanted to be a writer. He wanted his tombstone to read, "They read my stuff!" But he was Errol Flynn, the guy who lacked focus and discipline, the guy who drank and caroused, the guy who ran off to Acapulco, and later to Jamaica, on a whim; the guy who spent a portion of each and every day in the ardent pursuit of female flesh.

Flynn had made his first buck from writing by selling short articles about New Guinea to the Sydney *Bulletin*. Influenced by Kipling and Robert Louis Stevenson, his early prose charmed the reader and painted vivid pictures. It took Flynn a year to write his first book, *Beam Ends*, released in 1937 at a tidy 241 pages. The book proved a critical and commercial success and led Flynn to begin another. In the meantime he was also contributing articles to *Photoplay* magazine and writing for other magazines as well.

As he began his second book, a novel, he had a lot going on, from a crazy wife to a six-day-a-week production schedule at Warner Brothers, to the development of the Mulholland property. Flynn brought his manuscript to Mulholland when he moved in late in 1941. For a year, Mary Ann Hyde typed up his scribblings. "I write my stuff in long-hand," he said. "It is the sloppiest copy you ever saw."[92] Then came the little matter of the rape trials of 1942 and 1943, and Flynn put his novel away but penned a tribute to John Barrymore that he submitted to *The New Yorker*—which rejected it; a stinging blow to one Hollywood star writing of another.

Flynn picked up his novel again after he'd begun dating Nora Eddington, who took on the task of typing Flynn's copy. Over the years the book went through a number of titles until Flynn settled on, *Charlie Bow-Tie Comes to America*. The setting was the South Seas, with the hero coming to Hollywood to find fame and fortune. His publisher was Sheridan House of New York. After the rape trial, his mood turned darker, and he began channeling his frustrations with his studio bosses, with the press, and with life in general, into the writing of his novel.

He would say later that he did all his writing at the desk in his den. "There I sat often on weekends, when I barred the doors and wrote or tried to write."[93] The

During a break in production of the Warner Brothers drama, *Escape Me Never*, Flynn types a correspondence. By this time he had given up on handwritten communications. His faithful pal, Moody, seems keenly interested in what the boss will type next.

manuscript grew and grew, and the publisher became alarmed at what was being forwarded. Fearing libel suits at the thinly veiled Hollywood characters and situations, the latter half of the book was excised. Charlie Bow-Tie never did make it to America, thanks to Sheridan House, which released the novel, retitled *Showdown*, in February 1946.

It is likely that Flynn was devastated to see his work not just edited, but with whole sections deleted. He said later, "The book made no great impact on the field of literature, but it answered a need in myself."

He braced himself for the reviews, aware as he was that censorship had ruined the prose: "Critically, I am bound to be slaughtered. If the reviewers do like it, they'll probably say it was written by somebody else."[94]

The most interesting character in *Showdown* bears the unlikely name Cleo Charnel, a fiery blonde actress who—except for hair color—seems the spittin' image of Lili Damita, from her strange accent to her wryly arched eyebrow, cascading locks, undulating walk, and a "head held high and arrogantly." Except, in this alternate universe, the Flynn-based hero tames the Lili-like shrew, and at fade out it's clear they will live domestically ever after. This was probably the publisher's version, not Flynn's, because after the divorce Errol displayed no obvious affection for Damita at all, as she kept constant legal pressure on him through his attorney Robert Ford and through Warner Brothers to make alimony payments. When visiting with their son, Sean, the ex-spouses tried not to even look at one another.

With *Showdown* behind him, Flynn began another novel that may have incorporated Charlie Bow-Tie's Hollywood adventures, but the manuscript went nowhere. Instead, he turned to writing in a journal and penned some articles for *Screen Guide* magazine. He claimed credit for the dreadful screenplay to the independent film, *Adventures of Captain Fabian*, and also developed the script for his Italian epic, *William Tell*, a film that was never completed. Based on existing evidence, the screenplay as a writing discipline was not a strength for Errol Flynn.

Around 1957 Flynn signed a deal with G.P. Putnam's Sons in New York to write his autobiography. By this time he had spent 15 years living a life of purposeful debauchery and found his natural lack of focus compounded to such an extent that he simply could not do the job. He was a natural, story-telling writer, who with great frustration and sadness realized that he could no longer do the thing he loved.

California writer Earl Conrad helped Flynn finish the book that would become *My Wicked, Wicked Ways*, and it is assumed that the actual writing was all Conrad as spoken by Flynn. It is clear, however, that the exercise of spending months with Conrad dictating the book in Jamaica reawakened Flynn's enthusiasm for the craft, because his subsequent long, engaging letters to the ghostwriter included new passages and revisions to old ones. Flynn wanted to leave a good book for posterity and as honest an account of his life as he could allow, excepting that he did not admit to mean-drunk rages and dependence on cocaine and morphine.

My Wicked, Wicked Ways was published after Flynn's death and continues to be reprinted today. His tombstone does not bear the inscription, "They read my stuff!" but after a half century, people are continuing to read his stuff, making him, in retrospect, the successful writer that he always longed to be.

Sitting in his den at Mulholland Farm, near the desk where he had written it, author Errol Flynn points out the locale of his new novel, *Showdown*.

rely on injections of cocaine to ease the pain. He walks through his Warners pictures, his eyes dead, his delivery flat, for the next five years. He will rally briefly, as with his attempts at depth of character in *Escape Me Never* and *Cry Wolf*, but these will be panned. Where's the old Flynn? Where's the horse? Where's the sword? Where's the grin and the girl?

In her book, *Errol and Me*, Nora Eddington documents a Flynn both charming and cruel. They marry in 1944 in Mexico so that the child she is carrying will have a name.

little later he writes, "That which I had, my big house, my yacht, my bank accounts, seemed hollow. None of these could take the place of self-respect, which I had lost." He will say that he is not seeking sympathy, but rather, "I am only explaining why I was ready to blow my brains out."[95] He describes three successive nights spent at Mulholland, sitting on his bed, holding a revolver, at some points with the muzzle in his mouth. Unlike other Hollywood suicides, he will not pull the trigger. Not right away. But his decision to live on sets the course for the remaining 13 years of his life as he slowly, deliberately kills himself.

"It left me with a sense of abandon. I didn't give a damn what I did, where I went, what happened to me. I said to myself, Nothing matters now, do as you damned well please...."[96] The change shows in his face and work.

He will drink more, with vodka the liquor of choice. According to Nora, he will

Then the relationship becomes de facto, accepted in Hollywood without a press release, although he continues to deny that they are married. He adds a wing onto Mulholland House next to the den in 1945—another downstairs bedroom that includes a spread of mirrors on the ceiling. Above this room is an unfinished attic, accessed by an exterior staircase. In the attic is a trap door that opens into one panel of glass in the ceiling of mirrors. Two-way glass. Unlike the secret bar passageway leading to an equally

Flynn wrote this check to pay for part of the 1945 addition to Mulholland House that included a bedroom with two-way mirror and movie room downstairs, and a nursery and attic upstairs.

Errol Flynn turned actor-producer for his 1944 World War II drama, *Uncertain Glory*, playing a conniving French criminal. His strong and subtle performance, however, was betrayed by an uneven script. Flynn was involved in the casting of the picture and had an eye for the ladies (such as Warner starlet Faye Emerson, above) but not for screenplays. A lack of understanding of the importance of the script would spell trouble for his career down the road, in pictures like *Adventures of Captain Fabian* and *William Tell*.

secret closet of a room for voyeur pleasures, this new fea-ture of Mulholland becomes the talk of Hollywood. Supposedly Flynn uses this "gag" two-way mirror only once, on Bruce Cabot, who is furious at being spied upon—although many others will claim to be privy to the mirror and the antics of Flynn in using it.

The strange addition onto Mulholland House incorpo-rates an entertainment area downstairs; the bedroom with the two-way mirror can also be used as a movie theater (there is a projection room next door). And upstairs he adds a small nursery.

By 1946 Flynn has learned multiple times that there are consequences to the conquest of inexperienced teenagers. After the romance has flamed out, he's left with a wife, soon to become a plaintiff. Actor Robert Stack recounts a "miserable dinner" he spends at Mulholland with Errol and Nora:

"After a couple of hours, the dialogue rose to this: 'What can you do with a bastard like that?' Nora would demand.

"'It takes a bitch to know a bastard,' Flynn would respond.

"Finally, the battle came to an end, with Nora shouting, 'We don't have one damn thing in common!' As if on cue, Errol jumped out of the chair, ran upstairs, ran back down, and threw a monstrous rubber dildo onto the middle of the table.

"'We have one!'

"I went home."[97]

Flynn buys a new yacht, *Zaca*, and leaves his home to sail the Pacific and Atlantic. On one of his adventures, he discovers Jamaica. Suddenly Mulholland pales, and Flynn spends less time there. Alex also packs his bags now that the parade of women has stopped and the boss is cutting back his spending. Flynn hires Nora's stepmother, Marge Eddington, to succeed Alex.

On February 9, 1949, Louella Parsons announces that Nora will seek a divorce. Flynn is headed to Europe to make a picture, and Nora wants to strike before he leaves the United States. Flynn plays dumb on hearing the news and appeals to home, hearth, and apple pie: "If she wants a

The relationship between Errol and Nora was fractured from the start. She was a clerk, and he was...Errol Flynn. After the rape trial, he refused to acknowledge their relationship publicly, and the marriage was kept secret. Nora was a frequent guest at the house and played hostess at her "coming-out party" in 1945 (above), but she was never the baroness of Mulholland. (Deirdre Flynn Collection)

divorce, there isn't anything I can do but give her one. One thing I am grateful for is that I have wonderful children and a sweet and sympathetic mother-in-law."

Marge Eddington comes down strongly in Flynn's camp: "Mr. Eddington and I haven't seen Nora in some time. I don't mean we've deserted her, and I don't mean we don't love her, but I am devoted to Errol. He's been very kind to me, and both Mr. Eddington and I wish that Nora would reconsider this divorce action."[98]

The divorce is finalized in June 1949 and will leave behind daughters Deirdre (born January 10, 1945) and Rory (born March 12, 1947), children that Flynn adores. He can't get along with Nora (and certainly not with Lili), but he excels with his children, at Mulholland and at the studio.

Nora describes in detail Flynn's addiction to cocaine and morphine and his physical abuses of her while under the influence. She tells a story

Flynn shares an embrace with Ida Lupino in 1946 during production of *Escape Me Never*. Lupino was a frequent guest at Mulholland throughout the 1940s. One friend stated that she and Flynn "clearly adored one another." The porcelain beauty Lupino was one woman to whom Flynn was completely devoted, without even a hint of the underlying hostility he displayed toward his mother and wives. Perhaps Flynn's self-awareness that he was a marriage killer kept him from popping the question to Lupino—and ruining their otherwise perfect relationship.

that mirrors the description by Steve Hayes, who, as an aspiring actor, lives with Flynn at Mulholland for a month, later in 1949: "Sober, I've never met a more congenial guy. When he drank, very mean. Dreadful. He was spiteful to people. He'd say nasty things. For a guy who was full of hell and fun and seemed like a man's man, you hate when he becomes spiteful."[99]

Flynn is out of control. J.L. believes he can perform a rescue and puts Flynn back with a leading lady he likes a lot and with the director who has handled him best. Errol Flynn is cast in the post-Civil War western *Silver River*,

playing another anti-hero, as is now common in these days that are darkened by the emerging Soviet menace. Raoul Walsh will direct; Ann Sheridan will co-star, with able support from Flynn's pal of the Bundy Drive Boys, Thomas Mitchell. And after that, Errol Flynn will return to swashbucklers with the long-delayed picture about the great lover, Don Juan.

It seems like a wonderful plan, as J.L. sits in his office in Burbank; one that can't miss. But Warner underestimates his bad boy, and the plan will blow up and steer Flynn's career, and his life, straight into the rocks.

In a living room that featured originals by Gauguin and Manet, the painting placed front and center was the Flynn portrait by artist John Decker, a prominent member of Hollywood society since the early 1930s and a founding member of a group of broken-down, booze-soaked actors, writers, and artists known as the Bundy Drive Boys. Prominent in the group were John Barrymore, Gene Fowler, Thomas Mitchell, and W.C. Fields. Pat O'Brien referred to them as "the royal John Decker rat pack," and described them this way: "They claimed to be intellectuals, and yet their conversation was often about their victories over women, and their expensive ways of life."[100]

Decker liked Flynn and helped him acquire his Gauguin, Manet, and Van Gogh—or perhaps painted one or more for him, as Decker is thought to have been a magnificent forger. Decker completed the portrait of Flynn soon after the rape trial, and Flynn placed this cherished possession above the fireplace in the living room. That year, the Decker painting was featured in the press materials for *Northern Pursuit*, with exhibitors encouraged to offer prizes for a competition among local art students to reproduce Decker's work. In 1945 Ben Hecht wrote about the portrait for *Esquire*: "Decker not only gets a true likeness down—with one of the

swiftest, sharpshooting brushes in modern art—but he also introduces into his portraits a full Freudian biography of the celebrity involved.... Beauty, male or female, is a nasty handicap to an artist. Paint as you will, its conventional symmetric will dominate the canvass and spell dull flattery rather than art. In his portrait of Flynn, Decker has done one of his subtlest biographies. The handsomeness is there, to the last perfect curve. Without disturbing a line of the celebrated face, Decker has added to it the story of a troubled and ennuied soul peering out of weary eyes. Under the analytic Decker brush, the pugilistic Flynn

Above: Warner Brothers producer Mark Hellinger, fresh off his Warner Brothers bomb, *The Horn Blows at Midnight*, chats with artist John Decker and host Errol Flynn by the windows of the den. (Deirdre Flynn Collection) Below: The pressbook for *Northern Pursuit* touted a contest to recreate Decker's somber Flynn portrait for fun and prizes. (John McElwee Collection)

chin grows gentle, the mouth whose smile has enchanted millions, grows full of fretfulness. It is not a glamour boy who looks from the canvas, but a tormented fellow with a dislike for himself and the world."[101]

Decker and Flynn became partners in a short-lived Hollywood art gallery off the Sunset Strip that was managed by Decker, who died shortly thereafter in June 1947. His famous portrait of Errol Flynn is now in Jamaica and owned by Patrice Wymore. The portrait supposedly blew out a window during a Caribbean hurricane, but survived the ordeal with only minor damage.

John Decker, famous American artist, is seen here with Errol Flynn and the portrait of the star which he has recently completed.

Local Artists Paint Flynn's Portrait... Best Works Auctioned Off to Highest War Bond Buyers

★

Use this photo of John Decker's portrait painting of Errol Flynn as the basis of an interesting local bally. Invite the members of a prominent art school, or several individual artists, to paint a Flynn portrait in your lobby, using the photo enlargement of the still above as a model. Announce a war bond auction in your theatre opening night at which the finished works will be presented by the artists to the purchasers of the largest amounts of war bonds. Get story and pictures in local papers.

Order "Still TM A7x"—10c—from Campaign Editor, 321 W. 44 St., N.Y. 18

World War II hit Europe and the Pacific like a California brushfire. Errol Flynn tried to enlist in 1942 only to be turned away for medical reasons that included malaria and T.B. He traveled to Washington, D.C., on appeal and received no help. He ended up at Johns Hopkins in Baltimore, where he was diagnosed with an enlarged heart. James Stewart, Tyrone Power, Robert Montgomery, and others went to fight in the war—even Flynn's pal Bruce Cabot. And the screen's greatest adventure hero, in the prime of his life at age 33, remained home and instead spent his time fighting the law in a courtroom. "Everybody else was in this up to their necks," he said, "and I hadn't been able to find anything to do. No place to fit in. Nothing that I felt would do anybody any good."[102]

In November 1943 Errol Flynn joined the USO and embarked on a 10,000-mile, six-week tour of the Aleutian Islands. The Aleutians had been making news since June of the previous year when the Japanese bombed Dutch Harbor on Unalaska Island. Japanese invasion forces captured Kiska and Attu Islands in the island chain, and it took nearly a year to dislodge them in battle conditions that proved brutal, including constant winds, enemy booby traps, and the loneliness of such a desolate place. A U.S. counterinvasion forced a standoff on Attu, which ended with a May 29 Kamikaze attack at a place later labeled Massacre Bay, during which 3,000 Japanese charged to their deaths, while only 28 were captured.

Since June the Northern Pacific chain had been quiet, save for the howling winds, and it was here that a USO Camp Show featuring Errol Flynn, Universal player Martha O'Driscoll, singer Ruth Carrell, guitarist Jimmy Dodd, and magician Harry Mendoza island-hopped among the volcanic specks of land, from Dutch Harbor west to Attu near the mainland of the Soviet Union. Before the first stop, a commander warned, "They feel out of touch with the whole world. They hate themselves. Hate each other. Hate everything."

The act consisted of singing, dancing, and comedy invented by the troupe. They performed up to five shows a day. Flynn appeared on stage to begin the show and recited the first lines of the William F. Service poem, *The Shooting of Dan McGrew*. "A bunch of the boys were whooping it up in the Malamute saloon," he would begin. "The kid that handles the music-box was hitting a jag-time tune." By that point the audience didn't know what to expect, and from the curtain behind Flynn, Martha O'Driscoll's shapely leg emerged and the men would erupt

in applause, which was supposed to buoy Flynn into believing they enjoy his poetry. "Back of the bar, in a solo game, sat Dangerous Dan McGrew, and watching his luck was his light-o'-love, the lady that's known as Lou."

The soldiers of Amchitka presented Flynn with a blue she-fox that he named "Tundra Lil." So it went as they hopped the islands, the troupe lavished with attention by men who "hate everything," and Flynn feeling like an imposter who must be resented by these servicemen. A look at the photos from the tour begs the question, "Why is this man smiling?" The answer may be found in the girl attached to his arm, Martha O'Driscoll.

O'Driscoll had kicked around Hollywood since the 1930s. For years she was linked to Warners stock player William Lundigan, but in 1943 she wed a Naval officer in a marriage that steered straight into the rocks. She was all of 21, just the way Flynn liked 'em, and trapped with Hollywood's bad boy for six lonely weeks.

In 1947, O'Driscoll finally filed for divorce from the Navy flyer, who in a cross-complaint said the Alaska trip with Flynn was "highly improper" and a reason for their failed marriage. Film historian John McElwee, host of the Greenbriar Picture Shows web site, states, "Most women realized that if they got involved with Flynn, Bruce Cabot would have been winking at them from the next booth at Ciro's. But on the road, you're Martha O'Driscoll, and you're far from home. There's no one to answer to, no one to pass judgment. Celebrities on long USO tours paired off and had affairs and then went home and forgot about it."[103]

Flynn chose not to mention the Aleutians in *My Wicked, Wicked Ways*, and O'Driscoll chose to forget her entire Hollywood career when she married a millionaire and retired from the screen three years after the Alaska trip. She did, however, participate in an interview with a magazine writer that became the feature article, *My Six Weeks with Errol Flynn*, in which she admitted to "the most poignant memories of my life." In short, what happened in Alaska stayed in Alaska, leaving behind only a travelogue of still photos showing Errol Flynn with a glint in his eye, and a flushed Martha O'Driscoll clinging to his arm.

Above: Flynn introduces the fencers at his party for Nora Eddington. As always, Moody the faithful schnauzer is not far away from his master. Opposite page: The host seems to want more action as the fencers chat after the match. Seated at right, chin in hand, Peter Lawford seems immensely bored with the proceedings. (Both photos Deirdre Flynn Collection)

Left: Among the guests watching the fencing exhibition with Nora are, seated left center, Gary Cooper, holding sword, his wife Rocky, in sunglasses, Helmut Dantine, seated on step, in sunglasses, and Raoul Walsh, wearing an eye patch in the background by the window. (Both photos Deirdre Flynn Collection)

Standing on heavy cables running a 12K to provide extra light on a cloudy day, Guido Martufi (as William Tell's son "Jimmy") and Flynn as Tell share a moment on location. Behind them loom the Alps of northern Italy, near the Swiss border. Flynn's independent production of *William Tell*, which began production and then closed down in summer 1953 would be his Waterloo as an actor, writer, and producer.

SEVEN: TIGER LIL'S REVENGE

fter World War II, television hits Hollywood with the power of a magnitude 8 earthquake. "It was no longer the Hollywood I knew," Olivia de Havilland will later remember. Humphrey Bogart grumbles, "No one in Hollywood knows how to have fun anymore except me and Errol Flynn." The moguls face the prospect of massive changes to the way they do business, as the habits of the American public change and fewer people venture to movie theaters, favoring instead the comforts of home as they tune in to black-and-white TV sets. The last thing a studio boss like Jack Warner needs to worry about is a contract player gone bad.

Early in 1945 the idea for Flynn to portray Don Juan had gained some traction at the studio. It is another of those bigger-than-life characters that only Flynn could play, like Peter Blood or Robin of Locksley, and given his life and loves, the role holds the potential to top even these. Flynn eagerly devours the first draft screenplay—and hates it. He sits with producer Jerry Wald and director Raoul Walsh and discusses changes, but that same month, March 1945, Hollywood's set decorators go on a strike that will last seven months, culminating in the Black Friday riot at Warners' front gate. Flynn goes on to other productions; Don Juan moves to the back burner.

After scoring a controversial hit with *Objective, Burma!* Flynn makes four more vehicles that take him to summer 1947. He enters the production of *Silver River* a drunk and, by some accounts, a drug addict. J.L. sends a memo to Flynn's agent, Lew Wasserman: "If Flynn is late, if liquor is being used so that from the middle of the afternoon on it is

impossible for the director to make any more scenes with Flynn…we must hold Flynn legally and financially responsible.… We will never again make pictures where Flynn or any other artist becomes incoherent due to liquor or whatever it may be."[104]

Around this time, Flynn calls Raoul Walsh to Mulholland and asks for help. According to Walsh, physical exams show that Flynn's health is shot, and he asks for Walsh's advice, which is simple: Clean up your act.[105] So Flynn takes the pledge, and *Silver River* commences production. His co-star is Ann Sheridan, another hard drinker and, apparently, a bad influence.

Studio executives devise a plan to keep Flynn away from Sheridan for the first three-and-a-half weeks of production to get as much in the can as possible. Shooting for so long without the leading lady means "jumping periods" from one point in the story timeline to another—which Flynn hates to do. Despite his grumbling, the production starts strong.

Screenwriter Stephen Longstreet says, "Raoul Walsh, who was directing *Silver River*, came to me and said: 'Kid, write it fast. They're not drinking, they promised Jack Warner that, but you never know.'"

Cut to six weeks later—after three weeks of togetherness for drinking buddies Flynn and Sheridan. On June 5, 1947, J.L. sends a telegram from the Burbank studios to Flynn on location:

DEAR ERROL IF THINGS I HEAR ARE TRUE I AM SURPRISED THE DAILIES DON'T LOOK GOOD THERES NO SPIRIT IN YOUR WORK YOU ARE DOING THINGS YOU SAID YOU

NEVER WOULD DO WHILE WORKING ON A PICTURE THIS ISNT FAIR TO YOURSELF THE PIC OR YOUR FUTURE AND THE PEOPLE YOU ARE WORKING WITH[106]

Longstreet finds Walsh "...tearing pages out of the script. I asked why and he said, 'Removing the chicken shit. The dialogue. Too much yak-yak.'" Longstreet says, "I knew then the picture was in trouble."

Silver River will set studio records for cost overruns and days behind schedule, which, according to Longstreet, forces "...the studio heads to declare *Silver River* finished. It is the only major studio film I know of for which there is no ending; the picture ends in midair."[107]

Just then, Damita subpoenas Flynn to appear in court on July 29, 1947, to explain why he has missed making alimony and child support payments. She wants records of Warner Brothers and Thomson Productions, social security taxes withheld, and the existing Warner Brothers contract. Flynn remains a bankable commodity for the studio, despite the odd scrape with the law and paternity suit, despite chronic drinking. At a time when Warners is divesting itself of aging stars, Flynn is given a gargantuan new contract covering 15 pictures in the next 14 years, to take effect January 1, 1948. The first three pictures will pay him $200,000 each, and he will be free to work outside the studio for one picture a year. This rich new contract should take care of Errol's money problems and his satellite wives and offspring, but Flynn simply can't clean himself up, personally or financially.

Her back purposely turned toward the dream team, a confident Tiger Lil awaits the beginning of a legal proceeding to nail Errol Flynn for delinquent alimony and child support payments. Attorneys Jerry Giesler and Robert Ford stand between Damita and a haggard Flynn.

Hoping for a career revival at MGM, Flynn poses formally in the living room for a movie magazine in 1950.

knocks the pretty girls for a loop, even when he is not trying to court them."[108]

Making *Silver River* has damaged the Flynn-Walsh friendship to the extent that neither man wants to repeat the experience with *Don Juan*. Nor does Flynn feel confident in the abilities of Negulesco. But Flynn's drinking buddy Ann Sheridan speaks highly of Vincent Sherman, who has directed two of her pictures. He's easygoing; he can put up with some booze on the set. Flynn requests that Sherman—who describes himself as "one worried Jewish boy" on hearing the news—be assigned to *Don Juan*.

Sherman remembers, "For the first three or four weeks, we just got along beautifully. He was on time, he knew his lines. He took direction beautifully, and even

Above: Flynn got along well with young Viveca Lindfors as they pose together early in the production of *Don Juan*. Right: After a long, hard seven months, Flynn and Alan Hale share a relaxed moment on the soundstage.

The contract is blessed by J.L., who has deluded himself into believing in a Flynn renaissance that will commence with the long-mothballed *Don Juan*.

Director Jean Negulesco has been recrafting the script to take into account the changing public taste in pictures. Don Juan will not be a "home wrecker" or "unnecessarily quarrelsome," but rather, "What gets him involved in love affairs and duels is his physical attraction, his legend, which improved on it."[109] On November 7, 1947, the offbeat Flynn drama, *Escape Me Never,* premieres in New York to critical pans that take aim at Flynn. Sherman claims that this event causes Flynn to fall off the wagon and sends the production of *Don Juan* to hell.

The Adventures of Don Juan production file tells a different story. *Don Juan* starts to lag not because of Flynn, but because of Vincent Sherman's ponderous pace as a director. The production manager grouses time and again that Sherman is dragging his feet. It doesn't help that Alan Hale, playing Don Juan's sidekick, is ill for the first three weeks of production, but they shoot around him and Flynn remains a model citizen. It doesn't help that Viveca Lindfors, the female lead, is on another picture for three weeks, then arrives at the studio and from the first instant becomes, not merely a queen, but, more accurately, a queen bitch. Flynn, to his credit, "jumps periods" gracefully.

Not three weeks but three *months* into production, Sherman finds himself 22 days behind schedule, and Flynn suffers an attack of hemorrhoids—which may or may not really be hemorrhoids—but which are a pain in the ass for Jack Warner and the other studio executives. Everything has been going so well with Flynn. The studio has been pushing forward with efforts to publicize the picture, making sure that photographers are around when Flynn's three kids visit the set—seven-year-old Sean, three-year-old Dierdre, and baby Rory. Why the wheels come off, they don't know. But suddenly Flynn is hitting the bottle hard and back on the drugs as well.

"It was an experience to work with Errol Flynn, in spite of the fact that he was drinking heavily," co-star Viveca Lindfors will later write (conveniently forgetting her own part in the saga). "After 3:00 p.m. he was out, and all the close-ups of the rest of us, the other actors, had to be saved until then. Saturdays were a total loss."[110]

Maureen O'Hara would share a similar experience a few years later on another swashbuckler, *Against All Flags.* While lauding his professionalism, she noted "one glaring inconsistency...Errol also drank on the set, something I greatly disliked. You couldn't stop him; Errol did whatever he liked."[111]

Flynn's drinking weighs down productions for the prime years of his career and becomes a key factor in the production of *Don Juan,* as it lumbers on for seven months. At one point even Vince Sherman breaks down, and who should come in to pinch-hit but Raoul Walsh.

When shooting finally, mercifully, ends, Errol and Nora head to *Zaca* for a cruise that is to be covered by Hollywood features writer Sara Hamilton. The trip soon turns into a running Flynn vs. Flynn battle of such horrific proportions that Hamilton can find no angle for a story. The investment by *Photoplay* magazine is returned only in an uninteresting December 1948 two-page photo travelogue with captions. And no one looks happy.

As Warner Brothers' big Christmas release of 1948, *Don Juan* receives excellent reviews, but the studio's marketing campaign is disjointed and the box office just adequate. The handwriting is on the wall for budgets on Flynn's upcoming pictures. A few weeks later, Nora leaves him for singer and actor Dick Haymes, ending the six-year relationship. Suddenly his financial obligations to ex-wives swell to $6,000 per month.

But Flynn's new contract offers him a means of escape. Far off to the southwest from Muholland sits the sprawling MGM lot, home of the biggest stars and grandest productions. His pal Clark Gable has spent a career there and become king of the movies. Flynn exercises his contract option to make an outside film a year and makes the drive to MGM to begin *That Forsyte Woman* just in time for the studio's gala twenty-fifth anniversary. Flynn can be seen at official functions with the MGM all-star team and sitting in the official anniversary portrait. He looks as uncomfortable as he does out of place, but the intimidating setting pulls from him his first sober and focused performance in years.

After that it's back to Warners, to a B-programmer of a western, and back to the bottle. Nothing keeps him sober for long, although he recognizes that his time with MGM had answered a need to prove himself as a performer, and as a man. He asks for another loanout to MGM and has two films from which to choose: the H. Rider Haggard story, *King Solomon's Mines*, and Rudyard Kipling's tale of the British Empire, *Kim*. In retrospect, Flynn chooses unwisely, as he often does, when he decides upon the lazily paced, child's-point-of-view *Kim*. Flynn leaves Mulholland for a circuitous journey to India for location work, stops off in Paris, and there meets a girl he calls "a dream," with "the biggest pair of dark eyes I ever saw." So begins another inappropriate relationship, this time with an 18-year-old—a violet-eyed aristocrat of the Ghika dynasty, one-time rulers of Wallachia and Moldavia. Accent on the *one-time*, because now the Ghikas in general, and "Princess Irene" Ghika in particular, are out of power—and broke.

Just back from India and the production of *Kim*, Flynn lounges in his bathrobe and writes at the desk in his den at Christmas 1949. (Jack Marino Collection)

Still, Irene is born and bred as royalty and cool to his advances, and Flynn likes nothing so much as the thrill of the chase, no matter how long it takes. He courts her through his time in India, conquers her, and brings her back to Mulholland. Marge Eddington comments, "They are very well suited to each other." The romance makes all the papers, and a marriage is much discussed—Princess Irene Ghika is set to become Mrs. Errol Flynn number three.

Flynn is home, and some of the demons are gone. He's fit, he's got two MGM A-pictures to his credit, and a princess in the downstairs master bedroom. He hosts a succession of lavish and successful parties at the end of 1949 and the first half of 1950. Hedy Lamarr, who has just completed her siren's turn in *Samson and Delilah* at MGM—where Flynn is working—attends one of the Mulholland parties given for the Metro crowd. On a career high, Lamarr says, "I found my next script indirectly because of a visit to Errol Flynn's house." That script was *Lady Without a Passport*, which producer Jack Cummings offers to her down at the casino that evening.[112]

Despite Flynn's success on film and in society, he's restless, always restless. He heads off to Gallup, New Mexico, to begin a new western, *Rocky Mountain*, and falls in lust with his co-star, new Warner Brothers ingénue Patrice Wymore. Within days Flynn sends Irene packing and begins his pursuit of the tall, near-sighted, and quiet 23-year-old from Kansas. Flynn the leg-and-ass man will say later, "…she's got a fabulous pair of lean, sexy, gangly legs that puts her in the deluxe class."[113]

All the while, through his marriage to Nora, and his courtships with Irene and Patrice, he lives the high life and draws advances on his salaries. He throws lavish Mulholland parties, pays for the 120-foot *Zaca* moored at Newport, buys property in his new love, Jamaica, and travels, always eating at the finest restaurants and staying in five-star hotels. He has a sense of his debits and credits but leaves the details to his business manager, Al Blum. He is passive-aggressive about paying support to Lili for Sean and to Nora for Deirdre and Rory. And now in Nice, France, where Flynn makes the minor film *Adventures of Captain Fabian* as his 1951 loanout, he stages a media-circus marriage to Patrice Wymore, who returns to the United States to become the new mistress of Mulholland Farm.

"I really want to run the house like an efficient wife," she declares, and out goes Marge Eddington, despite her successful turn as manager of Mulholland for more than three years.[114] Pat finds it simply too strange, having an Eddington and a Wymore under the same roof.

Living at Mulholland with his bride, Flynn is fit and focused. His 1952 loanout is to Universal International for the swashbuckler, *Against All Flags*, with Maureen O'Hara. Then he begins what will be his last film at the Burbank Studios as a Warner Brothers contract player, the treasure-hunt melodrama *Mara Maru*, co-starring the latest studio hottie, Ruth Roman.

On January 18, 1952, the Flynns are at Mulholland when a winter storm hits. Three inches of rain fall in a day, causing flash floods that kill eight around Los Angeles. Water rages down from the mountaintop above the Farm, washing through the property. On February 7, Flynn sends a letter to his business manager, Al Blum, assessing the damage: the heater, water pump, and filter for the pool are "shot to hell," as is the heater in the furnace room. Says Flynn of immediate repairs to the heater, "I saved some dough on this job by having it done by a couple of Studio boys on their off hours, and got the whole thing fixed for $185, plus four jugs of bourbon."

In other damage, the brick wall outside his den is destroyed, the awnings to the upstairs bedrooms also destroyed, awnings to the tennis court shredded, and part of the roof peeled away.

Flying first class on an airliner, Errol Flynn and his 19-year-old princess are caught in a tense and unhappy candid moment. Irene Ghika's reign as baroness of Mulholland will be short-lived.

Three of Mulholland's most frequent visitors were Flynn's children, Sean, son of Lili Damita (born May 12, 1941), and Deirdre and Rory, daughters by Nora Eddington (born January 10, 1945 and March 13, 1947). Whereas Flynn acknowledged being a "lousy husband," he proved to be a diligent father when possible, given his busy shooting schedule and extensive travel for business and pleasure.

Errol started palling around with Sean when the boy was about eight and took him to the studio, to events, and adventuring on the *Zaca*. Flynn also grew close to both Deirdre, whom he called "Sam," and Rory, and the two or three kids would stay at Mulholland for a week at a time. When Flynn married Pat Wymore, he made it a prerequisite that she accept all his kids, despite continuing tensions with their mothers.

Flynn's ongoing money troubles forced him to live overseas, and the separation from all three children, particularly the girls, caused him heartache. He worried over them, called on the phone, sent a steady stream of letters and postcards, and begged Nora to send them over for time periods ranging from a week to a few months at a time.

On Christmas Day 1953, Patrice gave birth to the fourth and final Flynn child, daughter Arnella, and the three remained a family unit for the two most difficult emotional and financial years of Flynn's life. To her credit, Pat also helped to raise Sean and acted with him onscreen in "The Strange Auction," a half-hour episode of the syndicated television series *The Errol Flynn Theatre*, which also marked Errol's only screen appearance with Sean. By that time, Errol and Pat had already agreed to separate.

Flynn's return to the United States in 1956 allowed a happy reunion with his three older children, tempered by ongoing issues: his debauched health, his association with Beverly Aadland (who was only a few years older than Deirdre), and the lack of any sense of a home in Hollywood because by then, Mulholland Farm had been lost to Lili.

Life after Errol Flynn proved most difficult for the first and last of his children. Sean became an actor and adventurer who ended up as a combat photographer in Vietnam. In his book, *Two of the Missing*, Sean's friend Perry Deane Young said, "Flynn would always warn us—as a reason for staying in Vietnam—that you couldn't go on a combat assault in New York City. He meant there was no thrill 'back in the world' to compare with what we felt every time we got into a helicopter to be dropped into combat." This genetic disquiet, fearlessness, and thirst for adventure would soon cost Sean his life. He was captured by the Vietcong in 1970 and executed in captivity. Lili Damita Loomis, who remarried in 1962, three years after the passing of her ex-husband, spent years trying to find Sean, and died in 1994 refusing to believe he had been murdered.

Arnella became a fashion model and lived a life not unlike that of Gia Carangi, portrayed onscreen by Angelina Jolie in the biopic, *Gia*. Early success in front of the camera brought with it fast living and, in short order, cocaine addiction. Arnella ended up in Jamaica living on or near the Flynn estate and died there of a cocaine overdose in 1998.

Deirdre has spent her life in and around the movie business and contributed to a number of historical works about her father. Rory has been active in keeping Errol Flynn's memory alive through the web site www.inlikeflynn.com and the 2007 personal remembrance of her famous father and the home she shared with him. The title of her book: *The Baron of Mulholland*.

In 1952, his last year at Mulholland Farm, Errol plays with children, Sean, age 11, Rory, 5, and Deirdre, 7. They are walking on the small plateau above the lower pasture, with the tennis court behind them.

Contrasting views from the photo shoot of three-year-old Rory with her dad in the living room beside the Gauguin in 1950. First is the "look how she's grown" pose, then the official portrait of a happy couple, and then an improvised shot with a relaxed and proud father and a suddenly frightened little girl who's not quite sure what's going on.

Five years after the death of John Decker, his moody creation, the Flynn portrait, has moved from the living room fireplace, where it hung at an angle, to flush mounting over the mantel in the den. This is one of the last Flynn photos taken at Mulholland.

Flynn says that damage in the wine cellar "is worst of all, as far as I am concerned…where all the film is stored. Thank God, nearly all of it was stacked in racks and, therefore, above the water which came in. But two prints had been just recently returned and left on the floor to be filed with the others. After emersion, they were like jelly…and so scratched up as to be useless. It's not the actual monetary loss which, in the case of the black-and-white print, is about $480, and the one in color, $750, but the fact that I doubt if Warners' will ever agree to let me buy another print…."[115]

Flynn has collected his own films all his career, nagging his employers to sell him 16mm prints and, ultimately working it into his contract. The enigma emerges, the man who would stage slowdowns, inconvenience an entire cast and crew, make unreasonable demands, play sick, start drinking at noon, stumble or sleepwalk through his roles—and would proudly own prints of his titles, run them for family and friends, and loan them out to avid film collectors like Clark Gable and Lou Costello.

Errol and Patrice Flynn spent two years of relative happiness on Mulholland Drive that included premieres and other formal events.

At Mulholland during the production of *Mara Maru*, Flynn pens a long, melancholy letter to Nora in which he describes a visit by a Texas businessman interested in buying the Farm. Flynn says he has "felt for some time that perhaps a change of environ might be for the best." He gives the Texan a tour of the house, and they end up chatting by the bar. Here Flynn says that his mind had wandered back to a vision of a young Nora coming to him through the living room, dressed all in black—some episode from their earlier, happier times together. He admits to his ex-wife that maybe he's writing her a love letter and says that the memory of Nora in the house inspired him to turn the Texan down. "I allowed as how I'd just hang on awhiles to the li'l old joint because I couldn't think right off where else to go live."[116]

Flynn completes *Mara Maru* at Warners Burbank, then packs up with Pat and leaves Mulholland for Scotland and then Italy, where he will make a new Warner Brothers swashbuckler, *The Master of Ballantrae*. On December 9, 1952, he writes to Nora from Naples, "astonished" and frustrated to learn that Deirdre and Rory have been staying at Mulholland Farm for two weeks in his absence. He chastises her saying that "civility should have prompted you to acquaint me with the fact."[117]

Flynn will jump from Ballantrae to another adventure film, *Crossed Swords*, shot in Italy, and then stay in the coun-

Flynn displays a weary smile, vaguely focused eyes, and some serious bed-head as he arrives in London after seeing his family's possessions seized in Rome for unpaid wages on *William Tell*. He will meet with bankers here in a vain attempt to restart the production.

try for his next project. By then he is far behind in alimony and child support payments and can't return to the States for fear of his creditors. So the stay by his daughters at Mulholland will be the last habitation by any of the Flynns at the place they all love.

Errol, with and without Patrice, will embark on a four-year period adrift, lodging on *Zaca* and in hotels in Europe and on newly bought property in Jamaica, living paycheck to paycheck. He invests much of his remaining wealth in his own brainchild: an ambitious, independent feature called *William Tell*, to be shot in the Italian Alps. He hires respected Director of Photography Jack Cardiff to direct. He builds sets and selects a cast that includes his drinking pal Bruce Cabot. He shoots the film in CinemaScope. But when his backers withdraw, and Flynn runs out of money, no new funding sources emerge. Creditors appear on the scene, and Flynn drifts across Europe, begging anyone who will listen for funding to complete his film. Just as Pat gives birth to Errol's fourth child, daughter Arnella, Bruce Cabot files a claim against Flynn for back wages on *William Tell*. The clothing and personal belongings of Errol and Patrice are seized, along with Flynn's two cars. "I couldn't believe Cabot would do a thing like this to me," says Flynn. "No real man strikes at another through his helpless family—especially after he's been befriended for twenty years."

Back in America, another man does worse. Flynn's business manager, Al Blum, drops dead, and records reveal that he has embezzled tens of thousands of dollars of Flynn money.

Flynn is now desperate for cash and believes he will never again live in the United States. His new business manager, attorney Justin "Jud" Golenbock, places the following small, boxed classified ad in the Hollywood *Reporter*:

Nora is pressing Flynn for child support; Lili turns up the heat, demanding delinquent payments. Other creditors appear, including a Hollywood publicity firm that files a claim going back to 1950, when Flynn had been trying to get buzz going for his Republic production, eventually retitled *Adventures of Captain Fabian*, then filming in France. The suit against Errol Flynn and producer William Marshall claims that Flynn had agreed to pay $400 a week for publicity, but never sent a check.

In September 1955, Mulholland Farm is advertised at sheriff's sale. Flynn writes to Golenbock from Majorca: "…my main concern is the situation at Mulholland House and I would like to have your ideas on this and what has been done with this situation. Obviously the house is up for

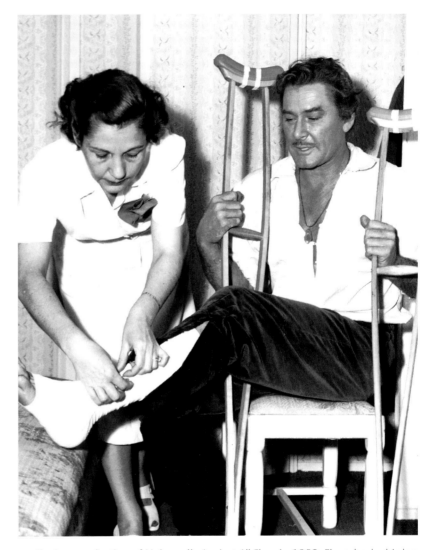

During production of Universal's *Against All Flags* in 1952, Flynn broke his leg while performing a stunt. It was one of many instances where he took chances physically and over the course of time his body was wrecked. Physical pain would be one reason he relied on vodka and morphine later in life.

sale and something must be done very quickly to save it or retrieve something from the ruins."[118]

On October 9, a municipal court judge awards Mulholland Farm to Robert McIlwaine and George H. Thomas, Jr., for their $1,988.62 claim against Errol Flynn and William Marshall.[119] Golenbock, on behalf of Flynn, scrambles to remove the artwork from Mulholland, pay the debt, and redeem the property. He approaches an interested party in San Diego, a man named Krady, about the purchase of Mulholland Farm.

Lili is closing in and backs Flynn further into a corner. At the end of October, he floats an idea past Jud Golenbock that they offer Lili 15 percent of Flynn's income for the next five years. In a letter to the attorney, Flynn makes a reasoned case for Golenbock to present to Damita: "Naturally if Lili is going to keep the dogs out after me then she makes it quite impossible for me to return to California. This does neither of us any good. By effectively preventing me from returning to California under threats of contempt of court and imprisonment she is hurting herself because naturally my value as an artist must automatically diminish....

"So what I propose is something like this.... If Lili will agree to call off the dogs then I will agree to some such deal that would guarantee her for the next five years 15% of my earnings.... Common sense, of which she must have some, especially in the financial matters, should tell her that this is the best deal she could possibly get. Certainly a lot better than she has been making out in the past 5 years and will in the next five if things continue as they are."

He adds in his own hand to the typed letter, "Of course the deal means a complete sign-off of all claims past or future by Tiger Lil."

Immediately below, in the same letter, the desperate Flynn states: "Please proceed immediately with the sale to Mr. Krady of the Mulholland house unless, of course this

After losing Mulholland Farm, Flynn lived a nomadic existence that included long stays in Majorca and Jamaica. Here he returns from Africa after *The Roots of Heaven* wrapped. Darryl Zanuck's secretary, Maggy Shipley, predictably succumbs to the Flynn charm.

deal [with Damita] could be made. Should I be forced to sell I want to try to get every bit of cash that is possible upon its sale naturally.

"There is easily 150,000 invested in cash in the Mulholland property. Irregardless of what it might bring on the market I would like to get the most cash possible and the sale made as soon as possible. Again this is in the event the settlement can't be reached with Lilly [sic]. Please advise me of the results immediately."[120]

The Krady deal falls through; the long-distance strategizing fails, and Tiger Lil gains her revenge. She claims ownership of a house that was never meant for her, a house she does not want, by paying $50,000 in liens late in 1955.

Flynn is down and out in Europe, but over the next couple of years, claws his way back to solvency. It is another period of upheaval. He buys real estate in Jamaica, and his third marriage crumbles. He takes meager jobs into 1957, when Darryl F. Zanuck casts him in a couple of films that lead Flynn back to the United States. He takes up residence in a bungalow at the Garden of Allah on Sunset Boulevard, a couple of miles from the Farm, and returns to Warner Brothers for the first time in almost six years to portray his hero, John Barrymore, in the biopic *Too Much, Too Soon*. His appearance is so shocking that few recognize him.

On the soundstage a long, shapely pair of legs catches his eye. Looking higher, Flynn sees a blonde chorus girl who is a self-described "early bloomer" of 15. The 48-year-old can't resist the chorine, Beverly Aadland, and they become constant companions in what will be the punctuation mark on a lifetime of inappropriate relationships. To go along with his conquest of an underage girl, Flynn manages one last adventure, chasing Fidel Castro around the jagged peaks of Cuba during the revolution that brings not liberation but Communism to the island nation in 1959.

On location making his last movie, *Cuban Rebel Girls*, he tells a writer, "I've been beating death for years, with the drink and the dames and the laughter and my way of living." Flynn has truly lived, from exploring hostile lands to rolicking through wars, making love to the most beautiful women in the world, gambling, flying planes, writing books, and sailing the seas. The least of Flynn may have been the movie star, and the most may have been the guy who domesticated himself enough to build a bachelor's

paradise in an unforgiving land, a place he knew as she went up must be temporary because Flynn subscribes to the idea that all things in life are temporary, or as Patton had phrased it, "All glory is fleeting."

While living with the energetic Beverly Aadland and observing the conquest of Cuba, Flynn begins his last creative enterprise. He accepts an advance from G.P. Putnam's Sons and sits down to write his autobiography—and gets nowhere, fast. He tells columnist Art Buchwald, "I can't write about myself because I lie to myself. I don't even know they're lies because I believe them." In a state of inebriated self-reflection, Flynn speaks of Patrice Wymore: "She claims she needs a career to reclaim her identity— whatever that means. The conclusion I can draw from this is that I make a good friend but a lousy husband."[121]

He is now estranged from all three of his wives.

Even though he doesn't believe in ghostwriters, Flynn hires a novelist, Californian Earl Conrad, to write for him in creative sessions that run many months in Flynn's sanctu-

Flynn's last love will be the beautiful but underage Beverly Aadland, whose shapely legs attract Flynn on the set of *Too Much, Too Soon*. Here, to make ends meet, she poses nude for a men's magazine after Flynn's death.

ary of Port Antonio, Jamaica. The stories pour forth, of ambition, greed, cruelty, money, booze, women, affection for his circle of cronies, anger at Mother, and a fierce dedication to—and grand disinterest in—acting. Through it all, the process brings to the surface vivid and romantic memories of his lost love, Mulholland Farm.

Errol Flynn will soon die in Vancouver, British Columbia, while in the process of selling his last important possession, the *Zaca*, in a desperate attempt to raise still more money. The post-mortem findings for this 50-year-old man include myocardial infarction and coronary thrombosis, along with coronary atherosclerosis, fatty degeneration of the liver, portal cirrhosis of the liver, and diverticulosis of the colon.[122]

As Flynn's body is finally beginning to cool from the cauldron that had produced him, Flynn's women begin a post-mortem catfight. Beverly Aadland, traveling with Flynn, insists that the funeral take place in Canada. Patrice Wymore insists it take place in California. Wymore wins,

and Buster Wiles travels to Vancouver carrying legal papers that clear Flynn's way across the border by rail in a twenty-five dollar coffin.

The passing of Hollywood's grandest swashbuckler sets off a flood of retrospectives in the national press, all of them wistful and affectionate, considering that this had been, at times, a nasty man often at war with reporters.

Columnist Louella O. Parsons writes: "There was a phase in Errol's life when he was married to Nora Eddington…when he fancied himself a country gentleman. He built a beautiful home atop of Mulholland Drive, surrounded by acres of land. I remember going there to a party and what a thoughtful, delightful host he was. It was the first of the lavish parties given in Hollywood and no expense was spared."[123]

Bill Slocum writes in the New York *Mirror*, "He had an epic home on Mulholland Drive and was inordinately proud of it. He lost it for taxes, being unable to keep up his standard of living, pay his alimony and also pay his taxes. He described the loss of the home by saying, 'One of my wives nationalized it.'"[124]

The end of Errol Flynn is marked a hundred times over that week in the same way—with a Flynn quip, a nod to Mulholland Farm, a string of colorful quotes from the ex-wives and film stars who had known him best, and toasts by hard-bitten members of the press who loved and hated the guy. All raise a glass to one who had made their jobs a lot more interesting for the quarter-century just ended.

Flynn remains today the sum of his parts; a charismatic man, an angry man, an artistic man, a perverted man, a beautiful

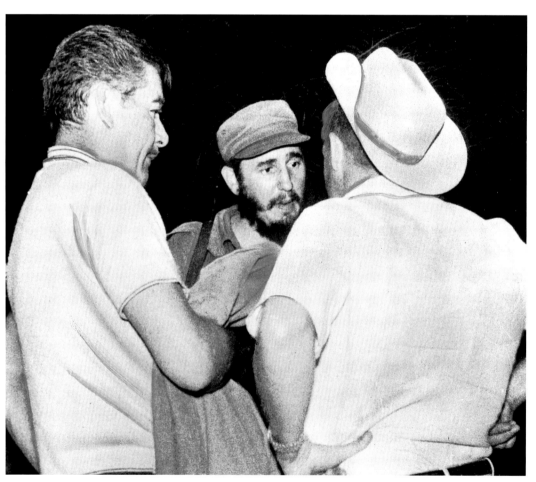

Errol Flynn and Fidel Castro share a moment. (John McElwee Collection)

Errol Flynn's last great adventure involved chasing "freedom fighters" (read: armed thugs) around the mountains and jungles of Cuba. He would make a couple of films about the experience and fancy himself a war correspondent one last time. (John McElwee Collection)

man, an ugly man, a graceful and a clumsy man. Like all humans, he experienced his triumphs and his tragedies, did his good deeds, and made his share of mistakes.

Legends pervade about Flynn's exploits. Most of the bad times are forgotten. His appearance and his voice remain in more than 50 motion pictures and they go on captivating people. He is spoofed in movies like *Robin Hood: Men in Tights* and redeemed in *My Favorite Year*. Sales of his DVDs soar, and books like this one continue to be written. And even with the passage of time, his grand mountaintop home, Mulholland Farm, remains a vivid memory, unforgettable, and a source of endless conversation to those who passed through its gates and explored the place to glimpse Errol Flynn's idea of heaven.

Back in the United States in 1959, Flynn's once-handsome face reveals a lifetime of physical and emotional pain as he stands with his daughters. Rory remembers greeting him at the airport. As he stepped off the plane, "...I was shocked. Suddenly, sadness came over me—this was Dad?...My Dad?? He looked ancient."[125]

In a magazine article, Flynn's friend Sara Hamilton said of Errol and his home, "Entirely free of the social bounds that encompass the lives and activities of big stars, he invites whom he pleases. It may be an actor out of work, or odd and sundry characters he may know only slightly."[126] This description fit young Ivan Hayes, a British subject who had set out for America at the end of the war, landed in Canada, and worked odd jobs in support of one goal: to be a star in Hollywood.

Hayes made his way to California and, late in 1949, found himself a passenger in a car driven by his girlfriend, Gloria, on his way up Mulholland Drive to a party at Errol Flynn's house. "I remember standing there," said Hayes, "looking at the faces of the people that were there. I saw Ida Lupino there. Bruce Cabot was there; I believe Big Boy Williams was there, Steve Cochran, Lawrence Tierney. Flynn knew Gloria—you don't date Errol and not go to bed with him. They were very, *very* friendly. He called her baby. He gave her a hug and there was a definite rapport."

The host was gracious with the newcomer. "Flynn treated me nicely. He was very interested when he talked to someone, learning about what they were and who they were." From Hayes, Flynn heard a familiar story, of a good-looking young guy who had knocked about, traveling the world and taking odd jobs, and had ended up in Hollywood.

For the next few months, Hayes shuttled between Los Angeles and Toronto. He met up with Flynn again soon after the star completed his studio interiors for *Kim*. Hayes reported that he was trying to find a sponsor so he could remain in the States. Flynn not only offered to sponsor Ivan, but invited him to stay at Mulholland.

Hayes lived at Mulholland Farm for almost a month, lodging in the aqua bedroom that had once been occupied by John Barrymore and by Buster Wiles. Hayes had an insider's view of Flynn within the confines of his home, and noted that he was "a terrible grump in the mornings" and ate kippers for breakfast. Flynn entertained many women, but wouldn't let them sleep over; Ivan heard cabs pull up in the night to take the women away. Flynn the drunk could turn nasty in a hurry, said Hayes, and his pal Bruce Cabot was a good deal worse.

"He was a prick," said Hayes, who related a story about a Flynn going-away party thrown at Mulholland in May 1950, before Errol was about to leave for location work in New Mexico on his new film, *Rocky Mountain*. At one point, Flynn and his cronies headed down to the casino. "Gloria and Steve Cochran and I were talking by the pool," said Hayes, "and Cabot said, 'Come on, Errol's going to stage a cockfight.' I said, 'You go on; I'm going to pass.' He said, 'What's the matter, pretty boy, you can't stand the sight of blood?' And I decked him. I went upstairs and I thought, 'Well, you just ruined everything. You struck one of Errol Flynn's closest chums.' I started packing my clothes. Flynn came up to my room and said, 'What are you doing?' I said, 'I'm leaving.' He was surprised. He said, 'Over a fight?' I told him I had hit one of his best friends. He said, '…who can be an asshole when he's had a few drinks. Ivan,' he said to me, 'for Christ's sake, don't worry about it. If you want to leave, leave, but don't leave because of that.'"

Within 10 days Flynn was gone to New Mexico to make *Rocky Mountain*. He took Princess Irene on location with him. They checked into the El Rancho Hotel, and here Flynn suddenly decided that his new, 23-year-old leading lady—blonde, violet-eyed, soft-spoken Patrice Wymore—would be an interesting conquest.

Hayes followed Flynn to New Mexico, trying to get his immigration problem resolved. Instead, it was Flynn who asked for help from Hayes. "What he wanted me to do," said Hayes, "was take Irene off his hands because he'd fallen in love with Patrice Wymore. He said, 'Stay over and get a room. I'll pay for it. Watch the movie and keep Irene occupied.' She was a princess! And they were engaged! And Irene was absolutely beside herself because he had gotten a crush on Patrice. I never understood that. Patrice was very tall, and in person she's kind of plain. I couldn't understand—Irene was 19, 20, a gorgeous brunette, and adored him, but he just couldn't keep still.... I think with Errol it's the chase. He always enjoyed the chase."

Hayes knew it was hopeless to have Flynn as his sponsor and left Gallup after one night. He would not see his friend again for seven years. When he did, "It was a very sad, sad time. He looked just dreadful. I used to go over to the Garden of Allah where he was staying, but I wish I hadn't. I wish I'd remembered him as he was."[127]

Ivan changed his name to Steve and went on to land minor parts in movies like *Titanic* and *The Scarlet Coat*. He wrote the original stories for the the Victor Mature film, *Escort West* (1958) and the H.G. Wells vs. Jack the Ripper sci-fi classic, *Time After Time*. Hayes also managed the famous coffee shop, Googie's, on Sunset Boulevard, and recounted his experiences with Flynn and others in the 2008 book, *Googie's: Coffeeshop to the Stars*.

Bruce Cabot and Flynn in happier times in 1940, when they were the young studs of Hollywood... years before aspiring actor Ivan Hayes decked Cabot for being a "prick" at a Mulholland party.

Only three days after Louella Parsons broke the news that Nora would seek a divorce from Errol, Flynn threw his last, and some say best, Hollywood party. He did it during the production of *That Forsyte Woman*, dubbing it his "coming out party" in the wake of Nora's decision to leave, and invited everyone who was anyone in Hollywood. George Jessel, the "toastmaster general," held court along with Flynn and Marge Eddington for attendees that included aging Hollywood royalty Gloria Swanson and Ronald and Bonita Colman, and the younger set, led by Cathy Downs, Susan Peters, and Shirley Temple and John Agar.

Flynn's current leading lady, Greer Garson, was instrumental in enticing many MGM personalities to attend, including Clark Gable, Van Johnson, Robert Young, Walter Pidgeon, and Eddie Mannix, along with such other A-list names as James Stewart, Dorothy Lamour, Ann Miller, Joan Fontaine, Jennifer Jones and David O. Selznick, Loretta Young, Jane Wyman, Dan Duryea, Rosalind Russell, Joan Bennett, Robert Hutton, Robert Stack, Audrey Totter, Alexis Smith and Craig Stevens, Virginia Mayo and Michael O'Shea, Lewis Milestone, and George Cukor. For comic relief, there were Jack Benny and Mary Livingstone, Judy Canova, and the Ritz Brothers.

Flynn gets chummy with starlet Dona Drake as writer Cobina Wright and a happy Shirley Temple look on. All study Smoky Flynn's Green Sheet for the white mice races. Later in the evening Flynn would make a pass at Temple in the steam room.

Flynn's cronies were on hand as well, led by Bruce Cabot, Alan Hale, Raoul Walsh, and attorney Robert Ford.

The L.A. *Examiner* said, "the view from his Mulholland Drive home is breathtaking. The valley lights resemble gleaming precious stones thrown on a black velvet cloth."[128]

Flynn ordered a bank of lights to be directed on the pool, and a marquee was erected over it. Huge water lilies floated on the surface, and an endless stream of bubbles wafted by. Guests dined on silver plates in a huge poolside tent erected for the event. The tent was large

Under an elegant tent on the lawn between the porch and the pool, Flynn orders a drink for Dorothy Lamour. The "front" door of the house is seen in the background.

enough for a fully stocked bar and formal tables, with catering by Romanoff's that included "brilliantly plumed pheasants" strutting their stuff on the white linens. A rumba band played steadily for dancing.

The floorshow was a campy production called the Arkansas Hillbillies, which included ad-libbing by Judy Canova and Harry Ritz. And of course there were the white mice races, for which Flynn wrote an elaborate and false historical retrospective and created names for 40 racing mice, including, Clark G ("Breaks and Cuts— Especially for Fillies."), Tiger Lil ("Ran Out When Backed with Smart Money—Mine!"), Jack Benny ("No Hope."), and Flynn's Folly ("Might Act Better if Gelded."). All these he put in the Original Smoky Flynn's "Never Loses" The Best Green Sheet handed out to all guests.

On the seamier side, Flynn was feeling none too kind toward "Lolly" Parsons for dishing about his pending divorce, so he hired a San Francisco transvestite to impersonate Parsons and made sure "she" was as offensive as possible in dishing secrets among the guests. After midnight, Shirley Temple and John Agar searched for Flynn to say goodbye, and found him in the steam room, drunk. "Come on in, Shirley," he called, looking about for Agar. "Just you." She declined. "Through the haze I could see his inviting expression turn scornful," said Temple. Flynn mumbled an insult, and Temple noted the incongruous end of her grand evening: "'Goodbye, kid!' he said, and waved me away with a sweeping gesture."[129]

The party lasted until 5 a.m., and several newspapers and magazines sent reporters and photographers. Photos taken after midnight showed a hammered but content Errol Flynn.

The night of October 14, 1959, Stuart and Suzy Hamblen, the new owners of Mulholland Farm, are at home on a cool and dead-quiet mountaintop evening. "The night Errol Flynn died," remembers Suzy Hamblen, "the whole house shook like crazy." The pressure regulator had gone bad, causing the pipes to vibrate. It will be the first of many strange occurrences at Mulholland House after the passing of Errol Flynn.

In some ways, Carl Stuart Hamblen is not dissimilar to Mulholland's previous owner. He is a talented and robust man's man, described by evangelist Billy Graham as, "rough, strong, loud, and earthy. Every inch of his six-foot-two frame was genuine cowboy, and his 220 pounds seemed all bone and muscle."[130] Hamblen is a movie actor, friend of John Wayne and Roy Rogers, and a radio personality, recording artist, and songwriter. For the past 10 years he has been an Evangelical Christian, thanks to a famous conversion at a tent crusade in Los Angeles that put the young "blonde, trumpet-lunged Graham" (according to *Time* magazine) on the map. After that, there would be no more gambling and boozing for Stuart Hamblen, who turns his considerable songwriting skills to gospel music.

It Is No Secret, a song inspired by a conversation with John Wayne, is credited with being the first gospel song to cross over to the pop charts. Another, *This Ole House*, becomes a hit for Rosemary Clooney and for Hamblen, and

Opposite page: A new regime takes over at Mulholland Farm; musician and radio star Stuart Hamblen poses under the two-way mirror in Flynn's downstairs bedroom, which now serves as the music room and recording studio. (Hamblen Family Collection)

is recognized as *Billboard* magazine's Song of the Year in 1954. He is such a songwriting talent that his work will be recorded by artists as diverse as Dean Martin, Elvis Presley, Johnny Cash, Bette Midler, and "practically anyone who ever did a gospel album," according to Stuart Hamblen's daughter, Lisa Hamblen Jaserie.

His past radio shows, *Stuart Hamblen and his Lucky Stars* and *Stuart Hamblen and his Covered Wagon Jubilee,* had been top-rated on the West Coast. Hamblen uses these programs to tell spellbinding stories in his easy, homespun style—like his contemporary, Arthur Godfrey, and like Garrison Keillor today. With such wide media exposure, Hamblen is asked to run for the office of president of the United States on the Prohibition Party ticket in 1952.

The Hamblens reside in Hollywood, then Arcadia, and then Westwood (to be near their daughters at UCLA). In 1958, with the kids out of college, Suzy Hamblen begins a search for a new home for the family, hounds, and horses—the Hamblens raise prize racehorses. Lately Stuart has been disquieted in Westwood, and his songwriting has slowed to nothing. Suzy believes it's time for a change.

As she will later record in one of her short stories, or Serendipities, she opens the Los Angeles *Times* to look at real estate ads, and the first one she sees lists five acres on Mulholland Drive. She ventures up to inspect the property with the idea that she and Stuart can build a new house on this site. Then her eyes catch on the higher 2.5-acre lot and "a beautiful, big, two-story Colonial-type house sitting high on the hillside overlooking all of the San Fernando Valley!" It is Errol Flynn's place on two separate lots, with

Stuart Hamblen saw this view of Mulholland Farm as Suzy drove him over Mulholland Highway from Outpost. "Now there's a beautiful place," he told her, not knowing that he was looking at the house she wanted to buy.

the lower five acres, including the stable and casino, to be sold separately, and the upper lot packaged to include the house, pool, and tennis court. That day, Suzy Hamblen makes a commitment to purchase both parcels for $160,000, which annoys her husband. "I don't even want to see it,"

Stuart Hamblen entertains the assembled throng of children during his first Easter egg hunt. In the background, the French doors of the dining room are thrown open, as Flynn used to do during his Hollywood parties. (Hamblen Family Collection)

says Stuart Hamblen. "You bought it. You find a way to pay for it! Just count me out!" She manages to get him up there for a quick look, but his mind is made up.

A year of house hunting passes and no house captivates her like Errol Flynn's place had. She assumes that by now it's long off the market and doesn't have the heart to find out for certain. In desperation she drives up the winding road and sees a billboard at 7740 Mulholland Drive advertising lots for sale—the lower five acres have now been subdivided. She motors up Errol Flynn's long driveway, now an official street called Torreyson Place. To her amazement, Mulholland House is still for sale, the white gables visible up the ridge. She stops her car on Torreyson and prays for guidance, and then returns home.

That same day the real estate agent calls stating that she has been going through her files; she wonders if the Hamblens have found a place yet. Later that day, Suzy relates the story to Stuart, who now must agree—given her prayer and the sudden response—that he needs to at least give the place some consideration. Suzy Hamblen later writes about the day they decide to buy Errol Flynn's Mulholland Farm:

"The first time I had shown the house to Stuart, we had driven up Laurel Canyon to Mulholland, gone east one mile to Torreyson Place, then up one block to the gate of the house. That was from the back and there was no sweeping view of it. This time I used a little more finesse and suggested we go up Outpost and west on Mulholland Drive.

"On the way, at every house that had a For Sale sign, Stuart would say, 'There's a nice house. Let's look at that....' As we came along Mulholland where you could look out over the whole San Fernando Valley on the right, he looked up to the left at the panorama of green grass and trees sloping up to a tennis court and a wide hillside covered with blooming lavender lantana cascading down it, leading up to a big two-story Colonial house. It looked like an old-fashioned Valentine card.

"'Now there's a beautiful place,' he said. 'If we could find something like that, I'd be interested.'

"'That's it...the place we're headed for,' I said.

"'It is not!'

"'Yes, it is.'

"'Well, I'll be damned.' He stopped the car, got out and looked at it for a long while. He had committed himself."[131]

The corner lots on Torreyson and on Mulholland—prime frontage— are already sold, so the Hamblens negotiate for the remainder of the subdivision and the upper lot with the house and tennis court. They buy it all, 7.5 acres, for $180,000 and begin a 20-year run at Mulholland Farm, almost double the time Flynn had spent there.

Upon moving in, the family finds strange mementos of the Flynn years. Harve Presnell, actor-singer and future star of *The Unsinkable Molly Brown, Saving Private Ryan, Fargo,* and many other films and *The Pretender, Dawson's Creek,* and other television shows, spends a generation at Mulholland as the boyfriend

and then husband of Veeva Hamblen, Stuart and Suzy's daughter. "We took about two truckloads of empty bottles, mostly vodka bottles, off of that place when Pappy and Nana moved up there," says Harve of the ravine behind the house. "There were a *bunch*; I don't know how anybody could drink that much, but I know it's a fact because I was the guy who drove the truck and the guy who put most of the bottles *in* the truck. Flynn and his crowd drank and threw their bottles out the window and over the hill and we had a cleanup of major proportions."[132]

The house becomes the center of the Hamblen universe, including Suzy and Stuart's daughters, Veeva and Lisa, and many grandchildren. Kim Jaserie, Lisa's daughter, will spend her first 12 years visiting and playing at Mulholland. "It was a very special place," she remembers, "and it brought a lot of love and happiness to a lot of families. All the people that came up there—it was wild. It was indicative of my grandfather too. That home fit my grandfather's personality as much as Errol Flynn's, because my grandfather was very robust and wild in his nature...and it was kind of like it fit with his lifestyle in being able to bless other people with such an interesting place."

Wild indeed. According to grandson Bill Lindsay, "My grandfather loved to hunt. He came in late one night and

Luckily these children can't see back in time to the raucous Flynn parties of old. On a sun-drenched Easter, Stuart Hamblen plays Pied Piper to a throng that is eager to descend the tennis court steps on their way to the Easter egg hunt. (Hamblen Family Collection)

had a mountain lion he'd shot. He didn't know what to do with it, so he empties out the half-height [freezer] in the garage and sticks the mountain lion in it, then goes up to bed. At about six in the morning he hears a scream and crashing, and my grandmother comes storming into the room. She says, 'Stuart, get out of bed and go see what you did to the poor milkman!'

"He goes downstairs and the milkman says, 'I'm sorry, Mr. Hamblen. I opened up the freezer and it scared me.' There was milk, eggs, ice cream all over the floor. My grandmother says to Pappy, '*You* made the mess—*you* clean it up!' He started cleaning it up, and she took pictures of it."[133]

"It was basically a ranch," says Lisa, who with her mother raises prize Peruvian horses there, with Stuart reveling in the role of rural rancher. "We had horses in the pasture," says Lisa. "We had Old If, his hunting horse that he talks about in all his stories on the radio, in the pasture down there."

Harve Presnell characterizes Stuart's personality in a story about the burial of Old If at the Farm despite a county ordinance forbidding such burials: "I came up there one day and drove past Pappy sitting in his truck with a gun. He was looking out the window. I looked across the street and there were a couple of county guys sitting in their truck. I said, 'Pappy, what the hell's going on?' He said, 'I told those boys they're not digging up If. He's buried right here and nobody's going to bother him, and they turned off my water, so I turned it back on.'"

Lisa says, "Daddy didn't know there was an ordinance against it. He just buried his

beloved horse.... The city officials were friends of his and they didn't want the bad publicity." If's grave remains undisturbed, but make no mistake: Hamblen is indeed robust, and wild in his nature—and, at the same time, a good-hearted guy.

He invents the annual Hamblen Easter egg hunt for his small grandchildren, which grows into an important area event. Says Bill Lindsay, the first in the wave of Hamblen grandkids, "Pappy would invite kids—I had never even seen some of those kids before. Who *are* these kids? I had no idea. There were kids from everywhere. Neighborhood kids; I even think one time he opened it up to people on the

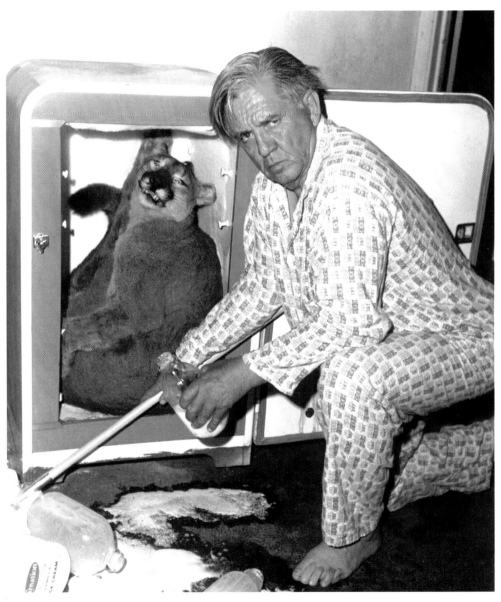

"*You* made the mess—*you* clean it up!" barked Suzy to Stuart, still in his pajamas, after he scared the milkman at 6 a.m. with a freshly killed mountain lion stored in the half-height freezer in the garage at Mulholland Farm. (Hamblen Family Collection)

Lisa Obee Hamblen Jaserie and son Billy feed the "prize" goat at the first annual Easter Egg Hunt in 1961. Every year, "I had to find a goat without horns," she said. (Hamblen Family Collection)

radio. It was amazing how many kids would show up for that thing." At its height, as many as 300 children congregate at Mulholland for the annual egg hunt, with the finder of a golden egg winning a live goat. Stuart and Suzy also host get-togethers and Bible studies and invite international students to the Farm once a month for 18 years.

"There were an awful lot of people up there from time to time," says Harve. "Reagan was there, and Duke [Wayne] came by. There was a lot of history in terms of people coming and visiting." Ronald Reagan had been a favorite of Flynn's and attended many dinner parties at Mulholland, and now visits the Hamblens to speak at a Young Americans meeting.

Stuart Hamblen hangs out with the country-western crowd. "Roy Rogers and Dale Evans were personal friends," says Lisa. "Johnny Cash they knew. One time Daddy was down performing at the Hollywood Bowl and told Mother that he had invited Buck Owens from Bakersfield to come up and Mother said OK. What she didn't know was that Owens was in a bus full of people, so she's greeting all these people and rushed up to the house and made a couple cherry cobblers and served everybody

GETTING MULHOLLAND'S GOAT

Errol Flynn, first owner of Mulholland, didn't have much in common with Stuart Hamblen, the second owner. But one Hamblen tradition that Flynn might have appreciated was the annual Easter egg hunt, or "roll," that grew from humble beginnings in 1961 as a diversion for the young Hamblen grandkids to an event that drew up to 300 children by the mid 1970s. Stuart and Suzy and their daughters, Veeva and Lisa, masterminded an elaborate ritual that included the planting of 60 to 70 dozen colored eggs around the lower pasture, which they divided into areas for the smaller and larger hunters. The grand prize was a golden egg. The Hamblens also released several dozen rabbits in the pasture, which Lisa had to procure. "You take what you can get," she said. "I got some angora, flop ears, brown, black, white, and just plain bunnies."

Easter traffic was heavy on Mulholland Drive for a decade and a half, with cars lining both sides of the driveway and spilling out along the edge of Mulholland. Egg hunters and parents gathered within the confines of the tennis court, and Stuart opened the gates for an hour of mayhem.

The grand prize, given to the finder of the golden egg, wasn't cash or toys. It was a live baby goat, which suited the rancher in Stuart Hamblen—but not all of his guests. As with the rabbits, Lisa remembers, "Some parents would see the gold egg and send their kids the other way."

"All the good people we knew came in with their kids," said Harve Presnell. "Those were the best times at that house—the Easter egg rolls."

Dozens of international students crowd the living room in the early 1970s; the Hamblens hosted these meetings monthly for almost two decades. (Hamblen Family Collection)

dining room and its designation, Men. All oddities of the previous owner.

Stuart and Suzy make few changes to the house. Lili had ordered the knotty pine living room to be painted white, but she left the den intact. The Hamblens love the knotty pine, and many other Flynn appointments, including the yellow bedroom and the aqua bedroom upstairs.

Two significant changes *are* made. Suzy Hamblen orders Flynn's bar to be taken away. She places an organ in that spot. And in 1967 a Christmastime fire destroys Rory's small nursery upstairs and burns through part of the roof. "We were on our way to Arcadia and met the fire trucks at the gate," says Suzy. "Our house was on fire and we didn't know it. But the fire trucks were there."

The Hamblens restore and enlarge the damaged nursery, which Suzy had used for a sewing room. "When they rebuilt it after the fire," says Lisa, "they made it a long dorm for all of the grandchildren."

Kim says, "Up in that room past the master bath—we used to go there and play dress-up."

Stuart Hamblen will write several of his most important songs at Mulholland—*How Big Is God?* one of the first after he moves in.

Lisa says, "My dad and mother loved the house. We called it 'the Castle.'"

Bob Lindsay says, "Nana and Pap picked us up after school, and we were there pretty much every day. It's not like this was my grandparents' house. This was like *our* house. We lived there."

Bob's older brother Bill remembers the sleepovers. "I have fond memories of being in the master bedroom there. The four of us were there. There were two cots, so some of us were in cots, some of us were on the floor, and we'd be at the foot of Pappy and Nana's bed, listening to Pappy tell

cobblers and root beer floats—all 60 or 70 of them." This open-door policy remains in effect for 20 years.

Suzy and Lisa raise their prize horses, and Stuart records his *Cowboy Church of the Air* episodes in the downstairs bedroom, right under the two-way mirror. The darker side of Errol Flynn is all around, and far from being offended, the deeply religious Hamblens find Errol Flynn's house oddly perfect.

"He was a little odd," says Suzy of Flynn.

"You'd wonder," says Kim, "why was this staircase here? Why was this trap door here? It reflected Errol Flynn's personality, because everything was beyond what you could imagine. From what I know about him, he was larger than life, and very imaginative, and the design was so different."

Kim's brother, Bob Lindsay, will spend years exploring the house as a kid. He will make his way through a crawlspace that runs the length of the roof line, from a guest bedroom on one side to the attic on the other, where he will open the trap door and peer down through the two-way mirror. He will try and fail to open a secret safe that Flynn installed in the floor of the downstairs bedroom. He will look at the door to the bathroom near the den and its designation, Ladies, and at the door to the bathroom near the

Stuart Hamblen was an admitted alcoholic and habitual gambler, and swore off both the night of his religious conversion in a hotel room in Los Angeles with Billy Graham in 1949. For nearly three years, until early 1952, Hamblen hosted the number-one radio show on the West Coast, *Cowboy Church of the Air*, using a formula that out-home-spun even Arthur Godfrey. But when a liquor company became a sponsor of *Cowboy Church*, Hamblen refused to go on the air, which forced the cancellation of his hit show.

Key leaders of the Prohibition Party heard Stuart Hamblen tell this story during a musical performance in Indianapolis, and approached him to become their 1952 presidential candidate in a year when Republican war hero Dwight Eisenhower was battling Democrat Adlai Stevenson. Hamblen had run for the U.S. House of Representatives in California's 20th Congressional District 18 years earlier but lost. Now he saw it as his public duty to try again, and Stuart Hamblen of Arcadia, California, accepted the invitation, running on a ticket with Enoch Holtwick, a long-time, unsuccessful Prohibition Party candidate for both U.S. Senate seats in Illinois. Also on the ballot that year was another Californian, attorney Vincent Hallinan of the Progressive Party, a colorful character in his own right who had been disbarred and spent six months in prison for tax evasion.

The campaign of 1952, set against a backdrop of the Cold War and fighting in Korea, was notable for the Irving Berlin *I Like Ike* campaign song, and for Richard Nixon's poignant Checkers speech, which would deflect him onto a path that would lead to his own election as U.S. president 16 years later. Here Stuart Hamblen found himself at the crossroads of history, mentioned with World War II hero Eisenhower and future U.N. ambassador Stevenson, and also with colorful Tennessee Senator Estes Kefauver and Minnesota Senator Hubert Humphrey, who were Democratic contenders in the primaries along with incumbent President Harry S. Truman. On the Republican side, California Governor Earl Warren—future Chief Justice of the Supreme Court and head of the Warren Commission investigating the death of President John F. Kennedy—battled in the primaries against Eisenhower.

Stuart's daughter Lisa enjoyed her father's lark in chasing the presidency, saying, "We thought, this is great, because the Prohibition ticket never wins."

On November 4, 1952, the electorate spoke, giving Eisenhower a near-landslide victory. But the Hamblens had an early scare that evening, based on returns from the Bible Belt. "In the very beginning," said Lisa, "when the first reports came in, my dad was ahead, and my sister and I were in a panic because we didn't want to move to the White House!"

Lisa and Veeva Hamblen needn't have worried. True, Stuart Hamblen did ring up 73,412 votes that year—which was only 34 million short of President-Elect Dwight David Eisenhower.

The Hamblens' open-door policy at stately Mulholland Farm continued for almost 20 years of egg hunts and family get-togethers. But in the last few years, the house and the neighborhood around it began to deteriorate. (Hamblen Family Collection)

and at religious events. In 1971, Stuart resumes production of his radio show, *Cowboy Church of the Air*, and records the programs in the music room underneath the two-way mirror. He activates a flashing light in the den to keep family members from wandering into his recording sessions.

In 1976 the Hamblens drive over Mulholland and down Laurel Canyon for the unveiling of Stuart's star on the Hollywood Walk of Fame. By this time, the neighborhood has begun to change, and the Hamblens entertain thoughts of leaving their beloved home of nearly two decades.

"Mother and Daddy moved because the area became really bad," says Lisa. "My husband and I had been here [Santa Clarita] for about five years at the time, and my parents had been getting police helicopters right over their heads, and bodies dumped on Mulholland Drive in front of their house. And houses had been burglarized everywhere; ours had not because of the dogs. Mother was alone when Daddy traveled, and the housekeeper wasn't there.... So with the bodies dumped and police looking for rapists, they just said, this is not a good place to be."[135]

Amidst plenty of buzz, the Hamblens begin showing the house to prospective buyers, which brings together the oddest couple on this or any other California mountain. Rolling Stones guitarist Ron Wood, friend of Rory Flynn from her modeling days, shows up at Mulholland right around the time that *Shattered* and *Beast of Burden* are charting. He receives a tour from Stuart Hamblen himself—a tour that features not the quaint, "colonial farmhouse" aspects of Mulholland. Rather, Hamblen goes out of his way to show Wood the secret passageways, the two-way

stories. He'd tell stories for hours. We'd just eat it up, and eventually fall asleep."

Suzy isn't the entertainer her husband is, but she is a vibrant force in her own right. "She was awesome," says Bill of his grandmother. "If we ever got into a fight, any of the kids, in the dining room, one whole wall was mirrors. She would stand both of us in front of that wall of mirrors, and have us recite Psalm 118:24—*This is the day the Lord hath made. I will rejoice and be glad in it*. And we had to say it until we were *glad in it*. Which wasn't long, because you'd say it with a frown on your face, staring at yourself in the mirror and trying to be mad, and you'd kind of laugh anyway."

Tulley Brown, another grandchild, says, "For us, it was the holidays. Any family gathering, any family *anything* for that whole period was at the Castle."[134]

Stuart and Suzy Hamblen are active and vital performers, appearing on national television shows, in parades, mirror, the viewing ports in the ceilings, all of which impresses the rock star very much. Not enough to buy the place, but Wood will reminisce about his trip to Mulholland Farm in an irreverent autobiography, *Ron Wood by Ron Wood: The Works*, released a decade later.

Another famous personality was much closer to actually buying Mulholland: star of *Jaws* and *Close Encounters of the Third Kind*, Richard Dreyfuss. "It was epic for me," Dreyfuss says of watching Errol Flynn movies as a child, and Stuart Hamblen is all too happy to take Dreyfuss through Mulholland and show him the Flynn touches.[136] Dreyfuss even draws up plans for renovations, but decides against buying because of the amount of work needed.[137]

In fact, Mulholland is destined to be owned by a musician, perhaps because music has been on the air at the Farm since its birth, when Flynn had fitted the entire house with speakers inside and out upon construction in 1941. Flynn's parties had always featured live musicians, or bands, or combos. Thanks to Stuart Hamblen, music has been more engrained than ever and isn't about to leave, even if the Hamblens feel that they have to move on. The first musician who sees it, Ron Wood, will say no. The second musician, who comes along right after Richard Dreyfuss, won't just buy Mulholland Farm; he'll be consumed by it, and a new band formed in Flynn's old master bedroom will go multi-platinum.

Following the Mulholland tradition, Stuart and Suzy Hamblen sit for a 1970s portrait using a leather easy chair in the den, with a dog at their feet, as Errol Flynn had done in this same spot a quarter century earlier. (Hamblen Family Collection)

RICK NELSON

© 1981 Capitol Records, Inc.

Playing To Win

 ON CAPITOL RECORDS AND CASSETTES
Produced by JACK NITZSCHE for North Spur Productions, Inc.
Management: GREG McDONALD

Rick Nelson released his last original album, *Playing to Win*, less than a year after purchasing Mulholland Farm. Says Joel Selvin, long-time music critic of the San Francisco *Chronicle* and a Rick Nelson biographer, "...on the whole, *Playing to Win* presented Rick in a thoroughly believable modern-day light, nothing ground-breaking but fresh and compatible with his essential character." Still, the album failed to capture the public's attention, which led in part to some lean years ahead at Mulholland.

The adventures of the Nelsons at Mulholland begin unexpectedly. "I remember him coming home one day," recalls Rick Nelson's son, Gunnar. "He said, 'I found the most amazing house. It's incredible and we're going to move there.' You have to understand—the house we were living in was in *Better Homes and Gardens*."

Gunnar's twin brother Matthew says of Mulholland Farm, "When we got it from the Hamblens, I remember it was pretty run down. You could look back on it and say, wow, that must have been somethin' in its day, but by the time we got there, the paint was chipping and you could smell the dry rot."

Eric Hilliard Nelson—America's teenaged rock-and-roller Rick Nelson—had seen the unveiling of his own star on the Hollywood Walk of Fame in 1975, a year before Stuart Hamblen.

Ricky Nelson had spent 14 years on the hit series, *The Adventures of Ozzie and Harriet*, which vaulted him to 30 top-40 hits by the age of 22. In 1959 he had reached his zenith as a young gunslinger in the Warner Brothers western, *Rio Bravo*, with John Wayne and Dean Martin. *Ozzie and Harriet* would continue for seven more years. During that time, in April 1963, he married Kristin Harmon, daughter of Michigan football star Tom Harmon and actress Elyse Knox, in what had been billed as the "wedding of the year." The run of *Ozzie and Harriet* ended after 435 episodes, in 1966, 14 years before Rick Nelson buys Mulholland. He had begun the show at age 12; he ended it a married man of 26, with most of his hits already behind him.

The challenges facing former child stars have been well documented in the past generation, but Nelson makes the transition out of the television grind without adverse effects. He is well mannered, armed with a long fuse, almost painfully shy, and remains every bit as quiet and self-effacing for the remainder of his life.

He returns to the spotlight in 1972, when his cynical and world-weary song, *Garden Party*, shoots to number 6 on the *Billboard* Hot 100. Recorded with his Stone Canyon Band, *Garden Party* is a thinking-man's view of a reunion concert at Madison Square Garden in 1971 that includes Little Richard, Chuck Berry, and others. Music-industry peers in attendance that night include John Lennon, George Harrison, and Bob Dylan. Nelson wears the fashion of the day, his hair shaggy, his shirt velvet and his pants bell bottomed. "No one recognized me," he says in *Garden Party*, "I didn't look the same." At one point, while playing his new material, boos rain down on him as the audience, there for a look back, appreciates neither his look nor his new music, and wants to hear only his old hits. "You can't please everyone, so you got to please yourself," is his response in the song. *Garden Party* reveals the depth and sensitivity of Rick Nelson, a performer then 31 years old who would "rather drive a truck" than feed the public's appetite for nostalgia.

Early in 1980, Rick learns that Mulholland Farm is for sale. He is familiar with the property because his father loved the place and had played tennis there with Flynn. Rick pounces on the opportunity.

After seven years on *The Adventures of Ozzie and Harriet*, Ricky Nelson lands a plum role opposite John Wayne and Dean Martin in *Rio Bravo*. (John McElwee Collection)

"It sells so quick," says Lisa Hamblen.

Nelson pays $750,000 for Mulholland Farm in April 1980, financing part of the sale through the Hamblens. Rick and Kristin move into the house with their four children, Tracy, the twins Matthew and Gunnar, and their youngest son, Sam.

"He was very proud of the fact that it was the Flynn ranch," says Matthew Nelson. "He was always kind of looking for secret passageways and things that he had read about in *My Wicked, Wicked Ways*."

Tracy Nelson realizes the mistake Flynn had made in 1941. "The front door was in a place where it shouldn't have been," she says, "so we never used it. Because of that I never really felt that the house had a heart; it had no center." Like all the owners and families who lived there, the Nelsons enter through the garage or the kitchen.

Early on, Tracy and her brothers notice a strange energy in the house. "When I was going to school," she says,

"girls would have slumber parties, but nobody would stay at my house."[138]

Gunnar says, "That house was seriously haunted. There was a lot of activity when we were up there. It kind of freaked a lot of people out. It didn't freak *me* out at all, but it's one of the things I remember most."

Adds Matthew: "I don't really know if it came from the fact that Errol Flynn owned the place and weird stuff happened up there back in his day, but it always felt like the house had a history. I wasn't a big fan of '40s movies at the time. He was a huge star and I knew who he was, but even if I had no idea that somebody famous lived in the house, I would have felt like there was something attached to it that wasn't normal."

The same month that he buys Mulholland, Rick Nelson signs a small but important two-album deal with Capitol Records. A year earlier he had hosted the popular *Saturday Night Live*, then with its original cast. After the taping, he had endured John Belushi's ramblings about producing Nelson's next album. Belushi is one-half of the Blues Brothers, whose album is then at number one. The private and careful Nelson bristles at the idea of being under the supervision of such musical hoi polloi, but nurtures an idea of his own: to be produced by John Fogerty, the genius behind Creedence Clearwater Revival. But as Nelson had demurred on Belushi's offer, Fogerty does the same to Nelson. Rick finds another producer and, in an excruciating process, completes the new album, called *Playing to Win*, his first new album in four years.

Nelson's sound has been described as rockabilly, pop, and rock, although he says with conviction on *Playing to Win*, "Call it what you want, it's alright/It's rock 'n roll to me." The album seems an effort, conscious or otherwise, to sum up his life to this point, with songs called, *Don't Look at Me* and *Do the Best You Can*. On the track, *The Loser Babe Is You*, Nelson seems to revisit the theme of *Garden Party*: "It's a loser's game, playing to win/It's all over before you begin/It's another day when you clear it away/It's just a lonely rendezvous with an old friend."

Late in the year Nelson hires a crackerjack media representative and begins promoting *Playing to Win*. One of a small army of reporters scheduling an interview is Regan McMahon, a features writer for a West Coast tabloid, *Bam*, who flies down from San Francisco. As she steps off the plane, Rick's business manager asks her to reschedule. She says no, so Rick Nelson leads Regan McMahon on a half-hearted tour of Mulholland Farm. She writes at the time, "The irony was almost too hard to take: wholesome-as-milk Rick Nelson the docent of one of Hollywood's most sordid secret playpens."[139]

McMahon remembers walking in the door and staring at a full-length oil portrait of Nelson as Colorado from *Rio Bravo*. Today, she describes a tasteful interior and lots of family photos.

In reality, Rick and Kristin's storybook marriage is a shambles—buying Mulholland is the couple's last hurrah and three months prior to this interview, Kris has filed for divorce. She is still living on the premises in Flynn's bedroom upstairs, while Rick claims the downstairs bedroom with the two-way mirror.

It will be a difficult interview—torture for a writer on assignment. "Of all the people I've interviewed in my entire career, he was the least talkative. I had pages and pages of questions. In this case, he was so untalkative, he gave so

Right above: Ricky Nelson, then 18, as the laconic Colorado in *Rio Bravo*. He told a reporter in Tucson during location work, "The fellow I play in the picture kills six or eight people. There's not much of that sort of thing in *The Adventures of Ozzie and Harriet*." (John McElwee Collection) Right below: Rick Nelson, new master of Mulholland, at the McAfee, New Jersey, Playboy Club in 1980. Leda Carmody, a fan and acquaintance, says, "It was my birthday. I went to the first show; it was all I could afford. Between sets I gave Rick a black shirt I had bought. When I told Rick and the guys I wouldn't be staying because we couldn't afford it, they treated my husband and me to the second show. Rick was wearing the shirt."[140] (Leda Carmody Collection)

many monosyllabic answers, that I could get nothing out of him. But when he talked about the house, he lit up at the thought of this famous guy [Flynn] who had all these parties right there."

One other thing makes an impression on Regan McMahon, now the long-time book editor of the San Francisco *Chronicle*. "Of all the people I ever interviewed, he was the most handsome. It was unbelievable. He was jaw-droppingly beautiful—and yet so shy. He was the opposite of someone full of himself. He seemed like a really nice, gentle guy. There was no edge to be provoked."[141]

But Rick Nelson is leading a life that in some ways parallels Flynn's. Rick's expenses exceed his income. In Kris Nelson's short time as mistress of Mulholland, she spends $100,000 on decorating. She installs, in various rooms, black carpet, white carpet, or red carpet. She paints the interior doors and some of the trim black. She fills the house with Victorian antiques…and contemporary artwork. She redoes the kitchen in garish colors.

In February 1981 Tom Snyder brings the *Tomorrow Show* to Mulholland Farm for a taping with the Nelson brothers, David and Rick. Around the same time Rick appears on the *Tonight Show* with guest host David Letterman, who jokes about Rick Nelson now sleeping under Errol Flynn's infamous two-way mirror.

But there isn't much that's humorous about Rick Nelson's life. He is paying a $6,000 monthly mortgage payment for Mulholland. Kris is spending manically. All four

Connecticut Farmhouse
3100 Torreyson Place
For Further Information Contact
Connie Nelson
788-0446

The divorce from Kristen Harmon Nelson is final, and Rick Nelson needs to raise cash. In 1983 he contacts his aunt, real estate agent Connie Nelson (ex-wife of Don Nelson, Ozzie's brother), to put his beloved Mulholland Farm on the market for a cool $1.3 million—$650,000 more than he had paid for it just three years earlier. (Robert Florczak Collection)

3100 Torreyson Place
Connecticut Farmhouse

5 Bedrooms , Maid's Rm, Formal Dining, Den, Breakfast, Pool, Tennis Court, Sauna, 6½ Baths

Errol Flynn's famed two story rambling estate above Mulholland on approximately three forested acres. Spectacular views from the San Fernando Valley to the Hollywood Observatory. Total privacy on gated drive. Stone-edged, black-bottom pool, winding path to tennis court. Gracious entertainer's flow. Four fireplaces, french doors, dormer windows. Thirty eight foot master suite, paneled den, dramatic formal dining room, very special children's bedrooms with nooks and crannies. Separate maid's quarters. Sauna. Zoned for horses.

General Information

Price	$1,300,000
Financing	OWC AITD or 3rd
Down Payment	$500,000
Escrow Period	45 Days
Bedrooms	5 + Maid's
Baths	6½
Heat	Forced Air
Sprinklers	Yes
Garage	Triple Att.
Sewer	CPL, SPT
Gr. School	Valley View
Junior High	Bancroft
Senior High	Hollywood
Lot Size	2.967 Acres
Zone	RE15-1
Taxes	Prop. 13

Room Sizes

Living	30 x 20
Dining	20 x 14
Den	19 x 18
Bedroom	38 x 27
Bedroom	24 x 17
Bedroom	18 x 17
Bedroom	16 x 13
Bedroom	14 x 11
Maid's	
Kitchen	15 x 11
Breakfast Room	14 x 8

788-0446

kids are in private schools. To maintain his family's lifestyle, Rick Nelson plays up to 250 concerts a year, in bars, county fairs, and trade shows. "I really like the fairs," says Rick. "I can get a whole wide variety of people—people who have never heard me, little kids, 10, 12, 13.… Their parents who bring them know me from a completely other thing. It gives me a good feeling when the kids accept me and the music."[142]

He loves his music; it's the music that makes him happy and keeps him sane, especially after divorce papers are filed. As Flynn used to do, Nelson is constantly hitting the road to raise money, and as Flynn used to do, Nelson accepts the attention of an endless parade of women. Rick Nelson doesn't have to make a pass any more than Flynn did; he needs only to make himself available for the taking.

Rick Nelson also tours to provide a geographical buffer from Kris. The estranged wife counters by sometimes traveling to his performances for in-person embarrassments or by having legal papers served before the curtain goes up. Alan Bush, Nelson's road manager, states, "The one time I heard him get really angry was when one of the lawsuits came in.… For Rick to throw out a couple of cuss words was pretty amazing."[143]

Mulholland remains a place that Matthew and Gunnar call home, even after the court orders them to live with their mother in Brentwood. "I went through a lot of hard times in that house," says Gunnar. "Our parents' marriage was falling apart not only dramatically, but spectacularly. They were doing it publicly, and it was awful."

With the boys all gone to live with Kris or her family, Tracy remains at Mulholland until she leaves for college and finds an apartment. Now Rick Nelson lives alone at Mulholland Farm, with only a Polish houseman staying in the far side of the house in the bedroom by the kitchen, where Alex Pavlenko and Marge Eddington had resided. For Rick Nelson, life is reduced to an exhausting schedule on tour, and periods of recovery at Mulholland.

Matthew says, "My dad had a fairly nocturnal existence while he was there, so the windows were taped up. He did the Elvis treatment on the windows in his bedroom. He'd just come in off the road exhausted and go in there and hibernate and come out at night."

Gunnar says, "To be honest with you, I think the house consumed my dad.

"After the marriage ended, he really did become quite the recluse. He woke up at four in the afternoon and walked around in his bathrobe and visited the Mr. Coffee and never really left the house. He had never been that guy before that house. He became the tin-foil on the windows kind of guy, and that was not who he was, but I can honestly say that there was an energy to that house that led to it."

Divorce proceedings drag on for more than two years, ending in December 1982. Rick Nelson faces staggering legal bills, alimony payments, and that ever-present mortgage. In 1983 he lets his aunt, Connie Nelson (ex-wife of Ozzie's brother, Don), put Mulholland on the market with an asking price of $1.3 million. In October 1983, following an interview, he stands on the steps near the pool and says to a reporter, "I don't know why I live here. It's much too big for me and I'm here all alone."[144]

At around this time, Connie Nelson takes artist Robert Florczak, a Flynn fan, on a tour of Mulholland Farm that confirms the hard times faced by Rick Nelson: "No one was home. She didn't want me to take pictures inside the house, because they were about to put it up for sale, but we went through the whole place. The house was surprisingly downbeat.… There wasn't much thought to the furnishings, especially upstairs. The boys had their guitars and amps up there, and my impression was that Rick Nelson's whole focus was his career and he really didn't care about his surroundings—as long as he had a decent home with a roof over his head, he was OK."[145]

Rick Nelson hits the road again in 1984, earning a half-million dollars in an exhausting series of play dates. He comes close to returning to stardom—Paul McCartney wants to produce an album for him, and play bass and sing background vocals, but Capitol Records says no. Tracy has become an actress, bringing new fame to the family, and Rick keeps touring. And the parallels with Flynn deepen: Nelson starts keeping company with a young model and actress named Helen Blair, 16 years his junior. Blair instantly becomes central to Nelson's life, as young Beverly Aadland had been central to Flynn's. Nelson's association with Blair alienates his mother, Harriet, and brother, David.

Rick appears on *Solid Gold*, *The Midnight Special*, and *Good Morning America*, and plays the Roxy on Sunset Strip. As he pursues his aggressive schedule, a new musical force arises back at Mulholland Farm. Says Gunnar Nelson, "Our mom wanted nothing to do with music at all. The fact that her two teenaged sons were so into music—she didn't want that around, so she thought by making us move our equipment out of that house in Brentwood because of neighborhood complaints, it would end the whole musical thing we were doing. But it kind of backfired on her because as isolated as the house was on Mulholland, it was a great thing for us to get away from our mom, keep our sanity, and weather a really tough divorce that was hard for the family. It was our safe haven.... We were able to put our instruments in the middle bedroom with the fireplace, and we rehearsed forever. We spent like five years there developing our sound, and it was nice to hitch a ride up to the house, and when Pop was in town visit with him, and get to work on what would later become the Nelson sound. If we didn't have that access, then there's no way we could have developed our music."

The boys enjoy the freedom of Mulholland, and Rick is forced out on the road to try to keep it. A deal nearly materializes wherein a wealthy Rick Nelson fan would buy title to the house and allow the Nelsons to live there rent-free, but nothing has been placed in writing. Meanwhile, the extensive touring causes the band to take a drubbing on commercial airline fares and schedules.

In May 1985 Rick spends $118,000 on a World War II-era DC-3, one of the most reliable planes ever built (but still a 41-year-old aircraft), to be used exclusively for touring. In August he flies up and down the West Coast for concerts with Fats Domino. In September he takes the plane to Memphis to participate in an all-star recording session that includes Jerry Lee Lewis, Carl Perkins, Roy Orbison, and Stuart Hamblen's old friend, Johnny Cash. At a media event for the

session, John Fogerty watches Rick Nelson make his appearance at the party. Says Fogerty, "What I perceived was a very shy man.... He smiled that nervous smile and went away."[146]

The next day will feature the Farm Aid benefit in Champaign, Illinois, and many of the stars in attendance in Memphis head there. Rick and his band decide to go too,

Graying at the temples and heavier after his sporadic periods of isolation at Mulholland Farm, Nelson still displays a love for the music at a 1984 concert. (Leda Carmody Collection)

but the DC-3 suffers engine trouble on takeoff, and the trip is cancelled. It will be the first of several incidents with the plane. One band member states, "Everybody hated it, but nobody would really listen.… It was like the main thing everybody always talked about."[147]

When Rick Nelson returns home, he finds that Matthew and Gunnar, now 18, have hurried to Mulholland to live with their father. We occupied the upstairs," says Matthew. "He occupied the downstairs. We were getting along great; everything was fantastic."

Regan McMahon, who had interviewed Nelson at Mulholland four years earlier, attends a concert during this time at a club in Berkeley. "It was an intimate setting. It seemed like his career was on the upswing; like he was going to gain back some rock fans. His voice was as strong and as sweet as ever. I had high hopes for the guy."[148]

Matthew agrees. "He was starting to get out of his shell; he was starting to get more social."

Christmas 1985 features a Mulholland Farm celebration with Rick, Helen, all four of his children, and a rare get-together with his mom and brother. "We had a really great party," says Matthew. "Our grandmother was there; our family was there. It was good for him; he felt really good. He looked like he was complete again. If I look back on it spiritually, it was kind of cool that he actually had some sense of familial closure and redemption."

On December 31, 1985, newsroom teletype machines pounded out the grim news of the crash of a DC-3 in Texas. The plane carried Rick Nelson and his band. The astonished Nelson children heard the news on radio and television—authorities apparently made no attempt to notify family members.

The next day Rick embarks on a brief tour to raise cash, and boards his vintage 1944 DC-3 with a revitalized Stone Canyon Band to play three dates: Orlando, Florida; Guntersville, Alabama; and Dallas, Texas. After playing Guntersville, the band boards the DC-3 on New Year's Eve and heads for Love Field in Dallas.

The plane crosses the border into Texas, and Dallas air traffic control hears a message from the 33-year-old pilot: "I think I'd like to turn around, head for Texarkana here. I've got a little problem."

That little problem is a fire that breaks out in the right aft section of the fuselage at 6,000 feet. In seconds, smoke fills the cockpit. The pilot—veteran of only 150 hours in this DC-3—realizes that he won't be able to use any of the vectors provided for nearby airports. He tries for an emergency landing in a farm field near De Kalb, Texas.

At 5:14 p.m., the plane makes a perfect three-point emergency landing in a field, but crashes into trees and rough terrain. The pilot and co-pilot escape through the cockpit emergency hatch, while the passengers are consumed in the flames filling the cabin—Rick Nelson, Helen Blair, four other members of the Stone Canyon Band, and their sound man.

Gunnar Nelson walks into Mulholland and learns of the plane crash from Dan Rather on the *CBS Evening News*; Matt hears it on the car radio.

The third owner of Mulholland Farm is gone. The National Transportation Safety Board suspects that the space heater had caused the fire: "During flight, the crew was unable to start the cabin heater, despite repeated attempts by the captain. Smoke then entered the cabin."[149] A rumor claimed that drug use had caused the fire—yet such a charge could have no basis in fact since there were no surviving eyewitnesses to activities in the cabin, and the fire was gasoline-fed, meaning that it must have emanated from the fuel line to the heater. The pilot had told the co-pilot at the crash scene, "Don't mention the heater."

Nelson is laid to rest at Forest Lawn Hollywood Hills, overlooking the Warner Brothers Studios, where he had made *Rio Bravo*, and where Errol Flynn's 17-year career had financed the building of Mulholland Farm, the place they both loved.

Gunnar says, "To this day, I remember when our dad was getting ready to go on the road with his big green suitcases at the bottom of the stairs, waiting for the car to arrive to take him to the airport. It's still in my mind seeing myself on the Flynn staircase looking down, waiting for those bags to be at the bottom when he came back from the road. It feels to me like he's, you know, still on the road and hasn't come home."

Matt and Gunnar live at Mulholland for two more months after Rick's death. Then late one evening, everything changes. Matt recalls, "It was the first and only time that I felt scared about the house. I remember walking in through the kitchen and looking into the living room; it's nighttime, and it felt incredibly foreboding, like it wanted us out." Says Gunnar, "It really didn't feel like home. It felt dark and oppressive and aggressive, and we packed up all our stuff and moved."[150]

Ultimately they would find fame and multi-platinum record sales beginning in 1990 with the band Nelson, then glam-rock, and, in the tradition of their father, they continue to write and perform. "A lot of the time we're playing the same venues he played," says Matt. "We performed at the Universal amphitheatre and I remember thinking...he'd be so proud if he was here."[151] Youngest brother Sam also works in the music industry, and Tracy's acting career continues on television and in theatrical films. She is a 20-year survivor of Hodgkin's Disease.

Weeks before performing with his brother Matt in a series of June 2008 Rick Nelson tribute shows in Atlantic City, Gunnar Nelson poses with the painting of his father as Colorado from the film *Rio Bravo*; this painting once hung in the entry way at Mulholland Farm. Of the lack of Nelson photos at Mulholland from this period, Gunnar says, "Mom and Dad were going through a divorce at the time, and I think people were so focused on staying sane through insane times that taking fun family pictures was not on their priority list."
(Photo by Liz Motley, courtesy of Gunnar Nelson)

No one will ever again live in the house that Flynn built. Its first and third owners are dead before their time, one by slow suicide and the other by recklessness. The second—and longest-running—Master of Mulholland is the last to pass on. No-nonsense Stuart Hamblen dies of brain cancer on March 8, 1989, 30 years after the night the pipes had first rattled at Mulholland Farm.

This aerial photo was taken by the Hamblen family when Mulholland Farm went on the market in the late 1970s. The compact nature of the house and wings is evident, as is the second-story renovation of the nursery into another bedroom, where hauntings would be reported by Tracy and Gunnar Nelson. Also depicted in this photo is the dramatic drop-off of the hillside to the observation deck, from which guests could watch Errol Flynn's tennis matches on the court below. (Hamblen Family Collection)

Authors' note: We set out to write an entertaining and factually indisputable account of the life and death of Mulholland Farm based on documented sources, credible correspondents, and new interviews. We planned for one short sidebar about paranormal activities at the house; sort of, "Ha, ha, isn't this weird?" But, after four years of research, we weren't laughing about the ghosts of Mulholland Farm, and our sidebar became a chapter.

Actress Hedy Lamarr, a frequent guest at Mulholland parties, writes in 1966, "I don't know who has the house now that Errol has passed on but I'd guess the Bacchanalian ghosts are still having a good time."[152]

Those ghosts do seem to be there all right, by 1966, but it's questionable about the time they're having. In fact, no documentation exists about hauntings at Mulholland Farm prior to October 14, 1959, but as noted, Suzy Hamblen certainly knows of Errol Flynn's demise—when the house announces it.

After Flynn's passing, Beverly Aadland had told the British tabloid, *The Daily Sketch*, "Of course Errol isn't really dead. His body is gone, I know, but nothing could destroy him. He's around. I know it."

In a similar vein, David Niven felt that Flynn's spirit was always hovering about, trying to guide him through the trying times faced by a Hollywood actor. Niven also believed that Flynn came to him in a dream and urged him to leave Hollywood and move to Europe.[153]

Stuart and Suzy's daughter, Lisa Hamblen Jaserie, would never see a ghost at Mulholland in her 20 years there, but is quick to note, "The house was spooky. There were a lot of spooky parts to it."

How aware are Stuart and Suzy of ghosts in their day-to-day life at Mulholland? Lisa's nephew, Tulley Hamblen Brown, says, "I do believe that Nana and Pappy, our grandparents, felt that stuff was going on there, but it's not like they wanted to sit all the grandkids down and say, 'Look, the house is haunted.'" He laughs and says, "They were always trying to brush it off.... I think they got used to it. There was no poltergeist activity, although one morning they woke up with the bed moved away from the secret passageway in the bedroom wall."

Harve Presnell says, "The funniest story about the ghost was that Pappy came in one day and said, 'There's a naked lady on the gate.' Nana said, 'You're seeing things. Have you been drinking?' He said, 'No. There's a naked lady hangin' on the gate, tryin' to get in here!' She said, 'Well, go take care of it.' So he went out and she had disappeared. That was a story they loved to tell."

Lisa's daughter, Kim Jaserie, says that certain rooms of Mulholland Farm would give her a terrible and uncomfortable feeling: "I never liked going through that area near the garage, that place where the water heater was and the bathroom; going through that drove me nuts. I always felt like something was there and I didn't like it."

Kim remembers having feelings of dread upstairs: "I had a hard time sleeping there, even though I loved the

Stuart Hamblen walked into the house to report that a naked woman was hanging onto the gate at Torreyson. "You're seeing things," Suzy told him. Stuart returned to the gate, and there was no woman to be found. (Photo by Robert Matzen)

house. The aqua room, the room that had the balcony, I didn't care for that one. I didn't want to stay there."

Kim's cousin, Tulley Brown, had similar difficulties in that bedroom during many family sleepovers. "We all had, at different times, different experiences. The room that bothered me the most was at the top of the stairs to the left—I always had a problem in it. One night in particular, I saw an energy or a cloud moving back and forth in the hallway. It didn't make me feel good; it freaked me out. I saw it consistently over the years."

Gunnar Nelson says, "There isn't a bedroom in that house that I didn't occupy at one time. We always would kind of like change rooms. It was very strange. When we first moved there and my sister was in high school, she had the room on the far left, above the den. When she moved out to go to college, that's the room Matthew and I took over because it was the biggest one and had its own bathroom."

Gunnar is describing the room off Flynn's master bedroom, which had been constructed as a nursery for Deirdre

Flynn. This room had been rebuilt and enlarged by the Hamblens after a fire one Christmas. Suzy Hamblen used it for sewing, and her grandchildren played dress-up there.

Tulley, says, "One time, all of us were playing in that room because that's where most of the grandkids slept when we were all together, and the light switch went nuts. It wasn't flickering as if due to faulty wiring; it went on and off several times, like someone hitting a switch, click-click-click-click. We ran out to tell our grandparents, and they said, 'Don't worry about it.' We were like, 'Well, if you say so, but....'"

Of this bedroom, Tracy Nelson tells Laurie Jacobson for her book, *Hollywood Haunted*, "All sorts of weird things went on: my shower door would open and close in the middle of the night; the toilet would flush; my shades would roll up for no reason."

In this room, Gunnar remembers, "We all had different experiences. I felt someone sit on my bed, like the bed indented, with the weight of a person on the bed, and no one was in the room at the time. I smelled perfume in that room as well, and it was thick."

"We used to smell this funky, cheap perfume," says Tracy, who senses feminine energy. "It didn't feel like a young, naive girl. It felt like a cynical presence."

With Mulholland Farm gone and no obvious way to investigate the haunting, the authors ask for help from Nancy Myer, a nationally known psychic investigator, author of the book *Silent Witness: The True Story of a Psychic Detective* (1993), a regular on Court TV's *Psychic Detectives*, and a respected consultant on FBI, state police, and local homicide and missing-person cases.

Upon inspecting photographs of Mulholland Farm, Myer says that the woman at Mulholland would take exception with Tracy's description of the perfume. "She wouldn't have thought of it as funky *or* cheap," says Nancy. "But it had a very strong odor, and I could see why people would refer to it that way." Myer feels that the woman described by Tracy Nelson had worked for the studio as a secretary or assistant and was in love with Flynn—unrequited love. In the course of her job she had spent a great deal of time at Mulholland, including periods of lonely solitude in the area of the nursery.

Sometime in the 1950s, according to Myer, after Flynn had left the house and the country, the lovestruck woman had commited suicide and returned to these familiar and comforting surroundings. Myer believes this energy is already inhabiting the house when the Hamblens move in.

The nursery that Errol Flynn built for his infant daughter Deirdre in 1945 was damaged in a 1960 fire, and the Hamblens built this larger room in its place. Here Tully Hamblen Brown reported lights turning on and off in the 1970s, while Tracy and Gunnar Nelson recounted ghostly activities in the 1980s, including window blinds that rolled up by themselves, the smell of a woman's perfume, and a presence that sat heavily, and invisibly, on the bed. Of the woman haunting this room, psychic Nancy Myer says, "I can sense her in the near part of the room, but she never goes into the far part of the room. When told that the room had been added on to much later, she says, "Well, that part of the room didn't exist in her day, which explains why she can't go farther." (Photo by Mike Mazzone)

Focus of the haunting: the addition that Flynn put on the Farm in 1945, including the area that had been used by the Hamblens as a recording studio and office for the music business, and by Rick Nelson as his master bedroom. Above was Tracy Nelson's haunted bedroom. The interior door at right led to Flynn's den, where Gunnar Nelson saw a man's face in a mirror. (Photo by Jack Marino.)

The woman must have been working at Mulholland in the period of 1945-50, after the addition had been built and prior to Patrice Wymore's appearance on the scene.

Myer examines photos of the nursery. "This room made her feel safe and comforted her, and she spent a lot of time in this room reading and just being quiet." Of Flynn's involvement with this woman, Myer says, "He saw her as someone who assisted him; he didn't see her as a desirable woman. But she was very much in love with him." Myer says she is confined to a certain part of the nursery. When told that the room had been added onto by the Hamblens after a fire, she says, "Well, that part of the room didn't exist in her day, which explains why she can't go farther."[154]

Paranormal activity is reported both upstairs and down. Says Gunnar, "I saw reflections of a man in the mirror right in the den, opposite the peephole in the ceiling where Errol could look down and see who was in the house because it had a really good view of the entire house. I definitely saw a man's face in that mirror a bunch of times."

Harve Presnell says, "There were quite a few things that went on in the entertainment area, where there was a fireplace and the music room. That's where a lot of *sightings*, so called, of the ghost happened."[155]

This is the 1945 addition to the house that featured the bedroom with the two-way mirror downstairs, a master bath, and the nursery upstairs. Kim Jaserie remembers an uneasy feeling downstairs in this area: "Where they had their recording equipment in the back of the house, I did not care for that, especially the shower area. Every time I looked at that...I couldn't sit still. I was outta there."[156]

Lisa says that the strangest occurrences of all centered in the attic, where the two-way mirror could be accessed by the trap door. Tulley Brown says, "My grandmother would work in Pappy's studio, and she would often hear footsteps upstairs in the attic. They'd go upstairs and find the door removed from the peep hole, and no one was up there."

"Somebody kept opening up the two-way mirror," says Lisa. "My dad and mother would nail it shut, and somebody would take the nails out, and this happened as long as they owned the house."[157]

Gunnar Nelson calls Mulholland "seriously haunted. The dogs would get freaked out all the time."

Not everyone who lives at Mulholland during the later years will experience the haunting. Gunnar's twin brother, Matthew, states, "I know Tracy used to get hassled all the time, but I really didn't. I had a girlfriend in high school and that's the place we used to go to have alone time. I got pretty good at jimmying the leaded-glass French doors in the living room and getting in. It was very convenient for me, his touring schedule and the fact that they were divorced. It gave me a place to go."[158] And for Matthew, there are no sightings of a ghost.

But Rick and Tracy Nelson will become well acquainted with the strange goings-on at Mulholland. Tracy recalls an incident for Laurie Jacobson: "One night I arrived home from work. It was dark. I looked up at the dining room and the light was on. There was a man standing in the dining room. I thought, 'Oh, Pop's home.' I went upstairs and called to him—no answer.... Then the phone rang and it was Pop calling from the road to say he'd be home tomorrow." Tracy told him what she has just seen, and Rick replied, 'Oh, that's just Errol.'"

Tracy describes two frightening examples of poltergeist activity in Lori Jacobson's *Hollywood Haunted*: strange cacophonies in other parts of the house, as if items are being broken. The first occurred while she was in her room and heard a racket directly below, in Errol Flynn's old den. "My father had a room below mine full of his gold records

In March 1987, author Robert Matzen stood by the pool and looked up into this dormer window, and thought he saw a figure peering out. Was it the ghost in the nursery, the one reported by Tracy and Gunnar Nelson? (Photo by Jack Marino)

and awards, all hanging on the walls," Nelson told Jacobson. "It sounded like whoever was down there was smashing Dad's gold records. I remember thinking, 'Oh my God, take anything, but don't take those.'"

She wisely chooses to stay upstairs and wait it out. "It was really loud, the house was shaking. It sounded like people were throwing things against the walls, breaking chairs and breaking glass. The sun finally went down. It had been quiet for a while and I thought it was safe to go downstairs."

Jacobson reports that, on the first floor, Tracy Nelson does not find broken glass or smashed furniture. "Instead," says Jacobson, "all the lights had been turned on. Two pet cats were in Rick's bedroom and the door had been locked from the inside. Nothing else in the house had been touched. Tracy decided then and there to move out."

A similar episode is experienced by Rick Nelson and Helen Blair and related to Tracy, who wonders if these chaotic events are meant to be communications. "My father's death was such a cataclysmic thing for the family,"

she says in retrospect, "…maybe the smashing was a warning… Who knows?"

The authors of this volume visit Mulholland in 1987, after it has stood empty for a year. Mike Mazzone feels nothing unusual in the house. Robert Matzen's experience is quite different: "I was standing by the pool looking at the house in dead silence in the middle of the day when I became aware that I wasn't alone. It hit me all at once, this uneasy feeling of being watched. I felt like someone was looking out from the second-floor dormer to the left. I *felt* something there—I think I *saw* something there—but then reason takes over to say I was imagining things. It wasn't until 18 years later when I read Tracy Nelson's account of her years at Mulholland that I felt relieved, like maybe I wasn't crazy."

Gunnar Nelson says, "If people told you, hey, it was all peaches and cream with that house, they'd be lying. There was a sexually charged, slightly aggressive, dark energy, if you weren't very, very careful." Gunnar's description perfectly fits the late Master of Mulholland, Errol Flynn.

Mulholland Farm is the only spot on earth where Errol Flynn ever settles in. It is his only home. He lives in other houses in other places, but never long enough to take root. Mulholland serves as his playpen and his refuge. If one chooses to believe in ghosts, then there is no more logical place for Flynn's energy to reside than here. And it's too intriguing that his face is seen in a mirror. First, Flynn states in *My Wicked, Wicked Ways* that he doesn't like to look at himself in the mirror. Second, during his life at Mulholland, he is known for his parties, and for looking at others through his two-way mirror.

Two months after the tragic death of their father, Matthew and Gunnar Nelson walked into the house, stood here with the kitchen behind them, and realized that they were no longer welcome. Matthew had not experienced any ghost activity during his time at Mulholland, but said, "I remember walking in through the kitchen and looking into the living room; it's nighttime, and it felt incredibly foreboding like it wanted us out." Gunnar described the house at that moment as "dark and oppressive and aggressive." (Jack Marino Collection)

Gunnar Nelson says, "That house was kind of like a

living, breathing entity. I had felt it at times when it seemed like a neglected person who just wanted a little love put into it. At times it felt like it was giving off a lot of positivity. The energy in the house was highly sexually charged. It just always was. There was always a really electric sexual energy in the house. It *might* have been the spirit of Errol; I really don't know."

Tulley Brown says of his experience in the early 1970s in the aqua bedroom, observing the movement in the hallway beyond, "After that one night and what I saw in that room, I don't discount anything that anyone says happened in that house."[159]

Two months after Rick Nelson's death, the Nelson twins notice a distinct change in the house. They walk in from the kitchen one evening and stare at the 30-foot expanse of living room before them, with the den beyond. Matthew, who hasn't been experiencing paranormal activi-

ties, says of his last night at Mulholland, "It felt...like it wanted us out."

"It felt dark and oppressive and aggressive," says Gunnar.[160]

Tracy says of the early years (at least with the ghost upstairs), "It had been playful," and, "To me, it was like having a pet." Then over time things change. "...after my father died...everything just turned ugly and scary in the house. My ex-husband always had a hard time believing any of this ghost stuff. After Dad died, we were removing some furniture and he went outside and refused to go back in. He told me, 'Something's in that house and I don't want to be anywhere near it.'"[161]

Tales of haunting end abruptly in 1988. Only the present owner, Justin Timberlake, whose house sits on the footprint of the Farm, knows if unusual occurrences are continuing at the property once treasured by Errol Flynn.

Less than two years after the death of Rick Nelson, Mulholland Farm sits deserted, the strip of grass that had once been trod upon by Hollywood immortals now scorched by the California sun. But *were* all of the inhabitants really gone? (Photo by Mike Mazzone)

In this view, the 1945 addition is seen through the gates to the tennis court stairway. (Photo by Greg Maradei)

ELEVEN: THE DEATH OF MULHOLLAND FARM

By the time that Suzy Hamblen had convinced her husband that they should purchase Errol Flynn's estate, lots on both corners of the property with Mulholland frontage had been sold. Flynn's 11 acres are now beginning to be whittled away.

During the Nelson years at Mulholland, the lower tract of land, formerly owned by Flynn, is subdivided, with access provided over a new right-of-way called Flynn Ranch Road. The barn is razed, and the casino building moved to a corner of the property and renovated.

Upon Rick Nelson's death on December 31, 1985, a portion of the $750,000 sale price for the house is still owed to the Hamblen family.[162] As this matter moves to resolution and the Nelson estate is settled, Mulholland House sits vacant. In 1987 the upper lot with tennis court goes on the market at a price of $1.6 million.

At this time, as Mulholland is shown to potential buyers, a new personality emerges on the scene. Aspiring film-maker Jack Marino is a transplant from Everett, Massachusetts, and—with a group of boyhood friends—a longtime admirer of Errol Flynn. Marino gets permission from the real estate agent to visit the house.

"I got into the house and took a lot of pictures," says Marino. "From April 1987 to May of 1988 I was going up there on a weekly basis. I'd go up alone; most of the time I didn't take my camera because I thought the place was always going to be there. I'd go up there and look the place over. If there were workers there, I'd drop the agent's name, and they'd let me in. Sometimes I'd call the broker and tell

him I wanted to go up there, and so if anybody called, he'd say, 'Yeah, I gave him permission.'"

After six months on the market, the price for Mulholland drops from $1.6 to $1.3 million. Marino remembers, "I happened to be up there one day and Tim Matheson was looking the place over."

On another occasion, Marino is surprised to find the gate locked, with a man walking around on the other side of it. Marino explains that he's a friend of the real estate agent, and the man states that he has just bought the house. They strike up a conversation, and Marino is invited inside. "He didn't know that much about Errol Flynn," says Marino, "so I told him some things. I took him around and showed him the different rooms, the two-way mirror, where Barrymore slept, and about the parties Flynn had.

The owner shows Marino blueprints for renovations he intends to make, extending the back of the house near the den and enlarging the second floor.

"At the end of the day," says Marino, "I asked if I could come back. He said, 'Sure, any time.'" Jack is greatly relieved that he'll still have access to the place.

As the months pass, however, the situation changes. Says Jack Marino: "I went up there in August of 1987 with my camera. I walked in the house, and the place was just about gutted. The living room still had paneling; some of the doors were off; the den was taken down. The entire second floor was gutted. You could see straight through from one side of the house to the other. I started taking pictures—I think I'm the only one with pictures of that time."

Inglorious last days for the living room: a double-wide pocket door that had been used to divide the living room from the bar now leans against the stud work of the far wall. Pickled-pine paneling from the den is stacked against the fireplace. (Photo by Jack Marino)

Marino asks the owner why the interior is being dismantled. "He told me he was putting the house up to code. New wiring because all the wiring was old and brittle. New plumbing, central air. He said he was going to clean the wood and then put everything back." A conflict with City Hall necessitates a halt to the renovations, Marino remembers. "By January of 1988," he says, "I was only going up there occasionally. It was very depressing."

On the first Friday in May 1988, Marino drives up to Mulholland to ask permission of the new owner to give a friend from Boston, also an Errol Flynn admirer, a tour that weekend. When he arrives at the property, Marino is met by a half-dozen workmen and notices that "the observatory window was out. The windows in the kitchen area were out. The chimney in the den had been taken down." Marino is told that all are rotting and must be replaced. He receives permission to bring his visitor from Boston, Steve Florentine, to the house.

That Sunday, Marino takes Florentine from Burbank Airport straight to Mulholland Farm. According to Jack Marino: "We drive up Mulholland and round the bend where you can see the house across the canyon, and I'm driving, and I want to point the house out to Steve. And it's gone. I've seen the house there for eight, nine years, and in that moment, it's gone. I'm thinking my eyes are playing a trick on me. I said, 'Steve, I don't think the house is there.'

Opposite page above: Houseguests sometimes got lost in the maze of rooms upstairs, which make more sense in the deconstruction phase. Ascending the staircase, Flynn's bedroom was to the right. Beyond it was the "haunted" fourth upstairs bedroom.
Below: Same view as page 126, with paneling and plaster removed from the downstairs bedroom. Sheer-wall blocking can be seen on most of the internal and external walls. The ceiling with the two-way mirror was at left; the spot where the mirror had hung is marked by the splash of sunlight in the ceiling. This room had last served as Rick Nelson's bedroom. "He gave it the Elvis treatment," said his son Matthew, covering the windows with tape and tin foil. (Photos by Jack Marino)

As we got to the front of Mulholland, the plateau was empty; I couldn't believe it. I drove up Torreyson. The place was torn down."

According to Errol Flynn, she went up fast, like the sails of a boat, and she has come down the same way, as if her sails have been struck. That day, Marino calls another acquaintance, Flynn biographer Tony Thomas, to tell him of the demolition of Mulholland. Thomas is a co-author of *The Films of Errol Flynn*, the first critical appraisal of the actor's career, plus other books including *From a Life of Adventure: The Writings of Errol Flynn*. Thomas is shocked to hear the news and asks Marino to drive him to the site. The next morning Marino, Florentine, and Thomas make the trip from Burbank over Barham and Cahuenga to tortuous Mulholland Drive.

"As we drove up Torreyson," says Marino, "there were two women getting out of an LTD. I asked Tony if he knew who they were. He said, 'That's Nora Flynn.' Nora was crying, very upset. Deirdre was very quiet, very upset. When you first meet Deirdre, she doesn't talk. She's a very quiet person. Nora said, 'Who would do such a thing? This is the house I came to as a bride. I had my first child here.'"[163]

They stand there surveying the scene a long time, and Marino documents the ruins in a series of photos. Deirdre Flynn snaps a picture of Tony Thomas, Jack Marino, and Steve Florentine standing by the living room fireplace, where the Decker painting had once hung. On a sunny day in May 1988, these five people are there for the end of This Ole, likely Haunted, House.

The owner who had ordered the razing of Mulholland House never does build there. The 3.5-acre parcel, including the pool, tennis court, and Japanese garden, is eventually sold for $4.3 million. Actress Helen Hunt then acquires the land and designs and builds a mansion there, nearly doubling the footprint of the old place. Later, Justin Timberlake will acquire it and continues to live there as of this writing. One particular attribute of the property attracts him: "Man, it's the reason I bought the house," he tells Matthew Nelson. "Best view on the planet."

Aside from the street sign reading Flynn Ranch Road, nothing is left to connect the place to the actor. The tennis court remains, although it's been resurfaced many times and hides behind fences and landscaping. The casino still stands, although it's been gutted and renovated, and moved 20 yards away from its original location to an obscure corner of the old Flynn property.

When asked if she ever visits 7740 Mulholland Drive, Stuart Hamblen's granddaughter, Kim Jaserie, thinks a moment. "After I heard that the house was torn down, I couldn't believe it. It was almost like a death in the family. That was a home that had an awful lot of memories, so why go over and see where somebody's torn down all those memories? The ground isn't important. The house is what made it special; the spirit of the people is what made it special; the history. I don't want to make myself depressed. It's almost like a gravesite."[164]

Another former resident does pay occasional homage at Torreyson Place, but not because of fond memories. For Matthew Nelson, growing up at Mulholland had been a test of survival through hard family times, and the spot where he had last seen his dad. "That whole era of my life, I guess you could say, was pretty tied to that house," states Matthew. "I drive past usually about once a year. I drive around the cul de sac. I occasionally see a neighbor who was living across the street." And his feelings upon hearing that the house had been demolished? "I was actually glad because frankly, I didn't have the best memories of it. For us, there was nothing great about that house."[165]

Opposite page: Two views of the den fireplace. Top, looking north toward the valley, shows the platform that held the downstairs bedroom and its two-way mirror. Bottom, looking east toward the mountains, with the den fireplace standing, shows the living room platform in the foreground and a shadow of the circular bar visible at extreme right. (Photos by Jack Marino)

Above: The day after the demolition of Errol Flynn's Mulholland Farm in May 1988, filmmaker Jack Marino visited the site with his friend Steve Florentine and Flynn biographer Tony Thomas. Here they pose at the living room fireplace, L to R: Thomas, Marino, and Florentine. (Photo by Deirdre Flynn) Below: By 1987, the lower pasture had been bulldozed and exclusive homes were under construction along a new private drive called Flynn Ranch Road. In this view, the Farm is still standing on the plateau above, and the casino (far lower left) has been moved about 20 yards to its new location and is undergoing renovations. (Photo by Greg Maradei)

Above: The house built for Helen Hunt, owned by Justin Timberlake, smothers the footprint of the Mulholland house. Below: The road at the right once was Flynn's driveway, which became a street called Torreyson Place. In Hollywood's golden age, Flynn, his cronies, house-guests, and partygoers, made a daily trek up and down this road to access the bachelor's paradise. Off Torreyson is the gated and highly secure Flynn Ranch Road, where several exclusive homes were built on the lower Mulholland Farm property. (Photo by Robert Matzen)

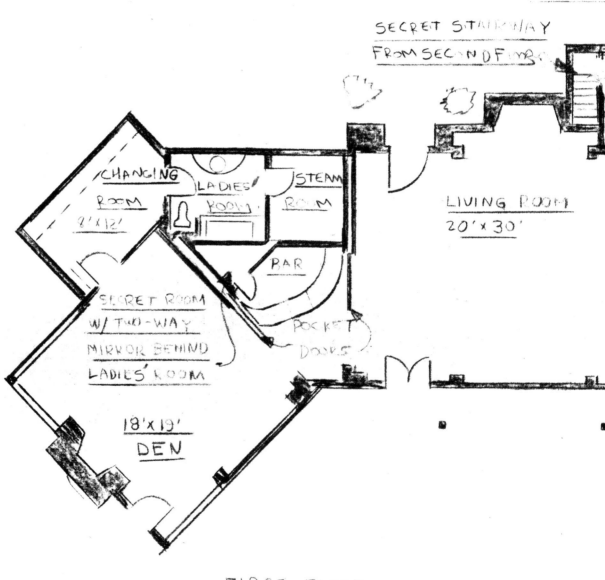

MEN'S ROO

SECRET STAIRWAY
FROM SECOND FLOOR

CHANGING ROOM
8'X12'

LADIES ROOM

STEAM ROOM

LIVING ROOM
20' X 30'

BAR

SECRET ROOM
W/ TWO-WAY
MIRROR BEHIND
LADIES' ROOM

POCKET DOORS

18' X 19'
DEN

FIRST FLOOR

Mulholland House: First Floor Plan

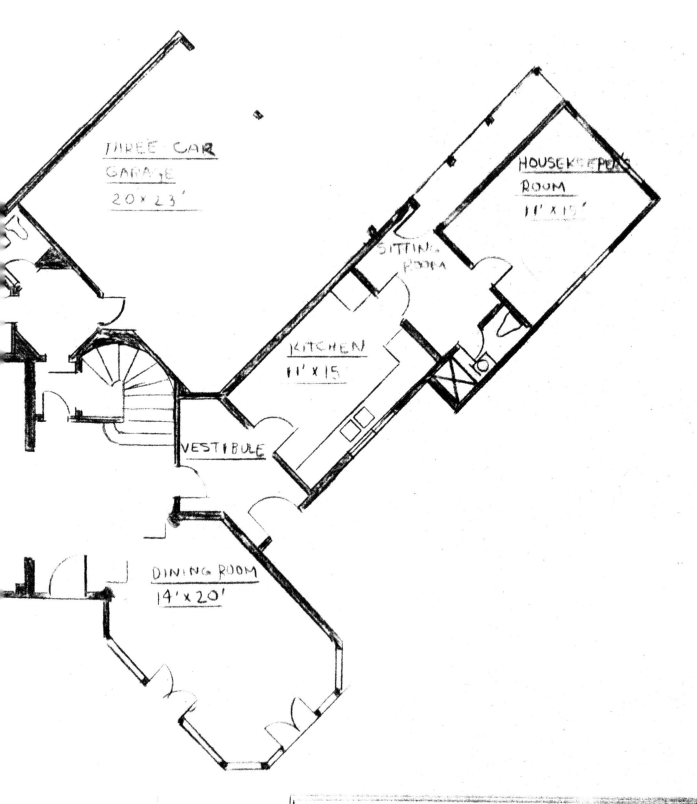

THREE CAR
GARAGE
20 x 23'

HOUSEKEEPER'S
ROOM
11' x 15'

SITTING
ROOM

KITCHEN
11' x 15

VESTIBULE

DINING ROOM
14' x 20'

ERROL FLYNN RESIDENCE 8-19-41
7740 MULHOLLAND HIGHWAY

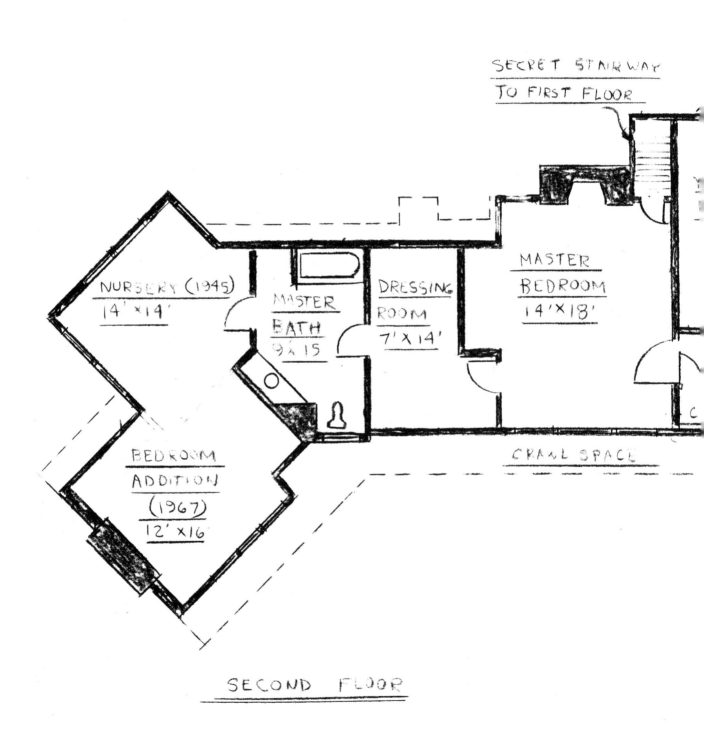

SECRET STAIRWAY
TO FIRST FLOOR

NURSERY (1945)
14' X 14'

MASTER
BATH
9 X 15

DRESSING
ROOM
7' X 14'

MASTER
BEDROOM
14' X 18'

BEDROOM
ADDITION
(1967)
12' X 16'

CRAWL SPACE

SECOND FLOOR

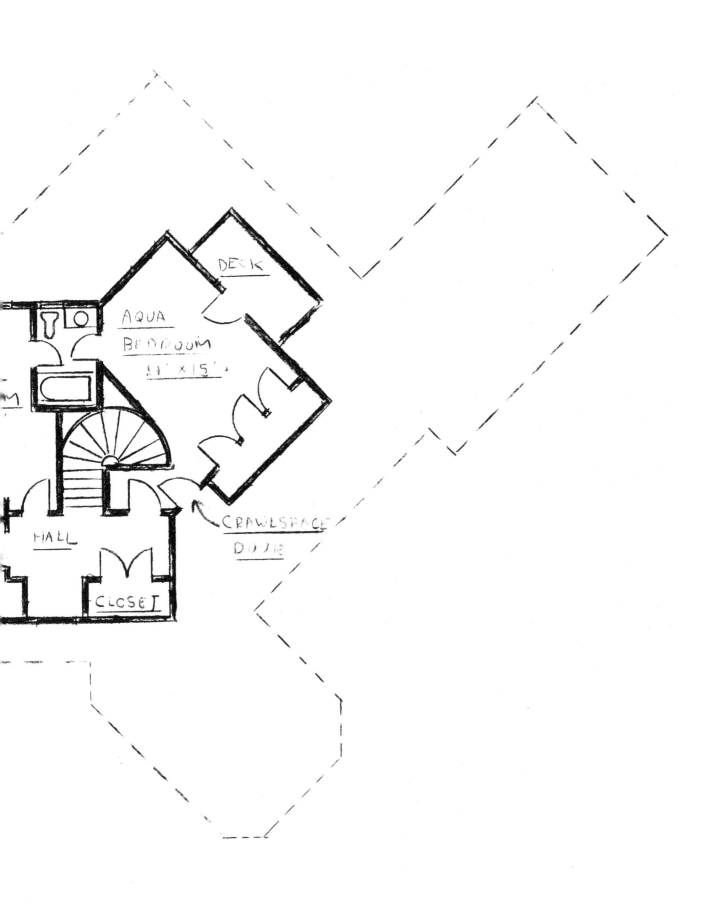

DECK

AQUA
BEDROOM
11' X 15'

HALL

CLOSET

CRAWLSPACE
DOOR

pack of reporters dogged Errol Flynn through life, one of them being Ginny Wood, who watched from a distance as the idea for Mulholland Farm took hold in Flynn's mind. Wood wrote of the Flynn property, "Many times I had seen it during the initial landscaping and leveling off of the home site. There it had always ended. Time and again, blueprints would appear, were discarded, and new ones begun." Finally, in 1940, Flynn decided to take a more active role in designing the house, and this floor plan resulted.

The look of the house reflected what he had seen of structures near the oceans he sailed, from steep-pitched roofs and dormer windows to a central spiral staircase. When he built the addition in 1945, he included with it an exterior stairway much like those seen on beach houses rising to a rooftop platform, except in this case Flynn's led to the attic and his special trap-door peephole. In terms of the interior, he could draw upon all the grand homes he had visited in the first five years of his career, from San Simeon to Pickfair. There he learned of viewing tubes permitting a glimpse down on the floor below, and the use of mirrors that weren't really mirrors at all, as well as secret stairways for discreet entrances and escapes, and a substantial crawlspace available with steep roofs with dormers.

The 1941 plan included the essentials: a living room, den, formal dining room, servant's quarters, plenty of bedrooms and baths, and a steam room. The 1945 addition provided an opportunity for more features important to him, including a movie theater, wine cellar, nursery, floor safe, and, of course, a new bedroom that could be spied upon.

By John Franchey

IT was one of those melancholy March nights that are the bane of the Hollywood Chamber of Commerce and the despair of improvident writers who are foolish enough to trek to Hollywood in March without an umbrella. The rain was beating a rhumba against the hotel window when the telephone rang.

"Bolivian Consulate?" a clipped voice inquired, clipped and annoyingly cheerful.

"No, the Aquarium. Ever try looking in a telephone directory? Not at all. Good night." And that was that.

Only it wasn't. The telephone rang again.

"Aquarium? The voice this time had a pseudo-celestial ring to it, the kind you get in Chinese-background pictures produced on Poverty Row.

"Yeah, what's on your mind?"

"It's about a couple of goldfish I've got. They're getting along in years and they haven't yet learned how to swim. It occurred to me it was about time they had."

Hunting and fishing are two of Errol Flynn's favorite sports. He is shown, bronzed by the sun, on a recent trip to Lower California with his paraphernalia.

Master of Mulholland Farm...

In his exquisite house high in the Hollywood hills, Errol Flynn talks to our reporter. This is the first interview Flynn has granted in eighteen months, making Franchey's story a real scoop!

The Master of Mulholland Farm, above; top, Flynn with his Doberman Pinscher in front of his sumptuous country-type house. The house is surrounded by hills.

Flynn, starring in Warner's "Uncertain Glory", is seen in the entrance of his grand home. A beautiful antique grandfather clock is in the background. He treasures his antique collection.

A close-up of the fine dry point etchings and gravures on the pickled pine walls, depicting various types of ships. This is a corner of Flynn's den. It's a cosy corner.

Magnificent tiles are set in maroon leather in the bar; these are small, but expensive. The mural decorations reflect the Spanish influence here. Magnificent retreat!

The July 1944 issue of *Screen Stars* magazine introduced America to Errol Flynn's unique home and included 10 photos taken of Flynn at Mulholland in late February 1943 by Warner Brothers still photographer Bert Six.

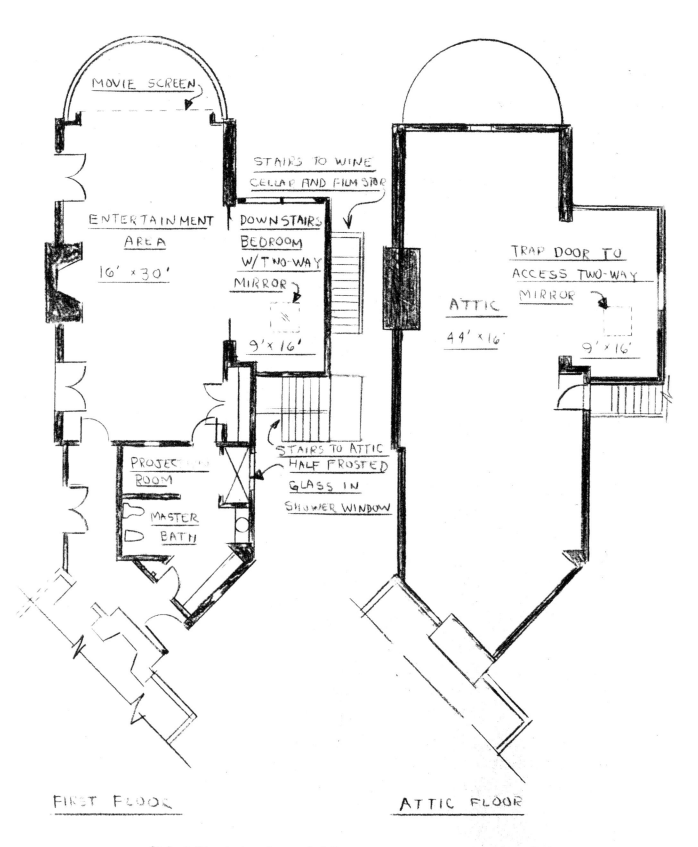

MOVIE SCREEN

ENTERTAINMENT AREA
16' x 30'

STAIRS TO WINE CELLAR AND FILM STOR

DOWNSTAIRS BEDROOM W/TWO-WAY MIRROR
9' x 16'

PROJECTION ROOM

MASTER BATH

STAIRS TO ATTIC HALF FROSTED GLASS IN SHOWER WINDOW

ATTIC
44' x 16'

TRAP DOOR TO ACCESS TWO-WAY MIRROR
9' x 16'

FIRST FLOOR

ATTIC FLOOR

EAST WING ADDITION JULY 2, 1945

Nora Eddington Flynn oversees buffet-style dining in the den during a party to introduce her into Hollywood society. Among the guests being served is actor Helmut Dantine (third from right), one of Errol Flynn's pals.

For the dining room, Flynn chose Chippendale furniture, and designed the space to include a wall of mirrors that "brought the beauty of the valley into the house." He invited guests to dinner often, from co-workers like Ronald Reagan to pals like Robert Stack to would-be employers like David O. Selznick. With the French doors thrown open, the dining room became a key element of party central for buffet-style food service. On an early date with Flynn, 18-year-old Nora Eddington dined with Raoul Walsh and his family. She said, "We had a delicious dinner by candlelight. The Walshes were charming. The talk centered mostly around the movie industry and I added little to the conversation. What I did say I carefully thought out first so that I wouldn't sound stupid."[166] When Flynn needed a room for a formal meeting, this was it, like those with Jerry Giesler, Bob Ford, Buster Wiles, and others during the rape trial. Linda Christian remembers "the quarreling, the foul language, the cigar smoke, the tension. Errol began tossing off brandy as if it were water. His hands were shaking, and he seemed to turn grayer before me. I felt great sorrow for him, and was overwhelmed with my inability to help."[167] Flynn didn't favor the dining room because of the great distance from his favorite spot, the den. Others disliked the room as well. Lisa Hamblen Jaserie remembers the wall of mirrors as one of the least popular features of the house. "When our family ate here," she said, "we killed ourselves to get on the side of the table where we were looking away from the mirrors so we wouldn't have to watch ourselves eat!"

As seen in this view by Bert Six taken in 1943 looking west toward the dining room, the 30-foot living room served as the center of socializing and conversation at Flynn parties, whether for the Master of Mulholland and one female guest, a party of six that had retired from the dining room, or 30 guests at a major event. At far left hangs Flynn's Manet, above a built-in radio set with in-wall speakers—an innovation in 1942. In addition to the "front" door into the foyer from the pool area, the living room featured two sets of leaded-glass French doors that could be opened for entertaining, with hand-blocked chintz drapery fabric that was repeated in the quilting of the couch.

In her autobiography, Veronica Lake related an attempted seduction by Flynn in the foyer (just beyond the folding room divider at the upper center of the photo). Lake said that it was the only Flynn party she attended and noted that the evening included nude swimming and luscious starlets, and she observed that "his clippings were not exaggerated." Errol Flynn parties *were* memorable. Still, Miss Lake grew bored with the proceedings. "Errol showed me to the door," she remembered. "He was handsome, that devil. He looked in my eyes and slipped his arm around my waist. His hand slipped down and clamped tightly on my rear end." Flynn recommends that they retire to his bedroom. She told him that she did intend to go to bed...her bed...in her home...alone. "He took his hand away," she said, "kissed me on the cheek and smiled." She said, "Errol Flynn was a gentleman. I remember one informal cocktail party where some guy was trying to put the make on me. Errol jumped right in and protected me like a father. I suppose when you have as much success with the opposite sex as he did, one turndown doesn't mean a thing."[168]

Above, looking east: Flynn paneled the living room in pickled pine with a faux beamed ceiling. At the back long wall he placed a formal fireplace trimmed in polished brass. Above the fireplace hung the portrait painted by John Decker. On one short wall in the room, Flynn placed his Gauguin and posed with it for nearly a decade of photographs. At the center of the room he arranged a sofa and two overstuffed chairs, with a coffee table in between. He designed pocket doors to be placed in the far arch so the bar and den could be closed off. Beyond the living room stood the curved bar. Right: A similar view 44 years later. The natural pine had been painted white in the 1950s by Lili Damita; "Mother never would have had it painted," said Lisa Hamblen Jaserie. Otherwise, the living room had not changed. (Jack Marino Collection)

Artist Henry Clive's rendition of the bullfight did not go well for the bullfighter, who is seen flying through the air, losing a shoe. Spectators painted into the arena gallery included Flynn and Raoul Walsh, among others. Suzy Hamblen said that the mural was still on the wall when she and her husband moved into the house in 1959, and they consigned it to an auction in Bullhead, Arizona. Stuart Hamblen had the bar removed and an organ put in its place.

"I think I liked my den best of all," said Flynn. "Here was my desk next to a window where the California light streamed in. I sat often on weekends, when I barred the doors and I wrote or tried to write. Nearby was a fireplace and wood was on the hearth; and when it was cool the logs burned and the room was aglow."[169] Of course, he needed that heat for those cold, mountaintop California nights with all those drafty windows—practically entire walls of windows in the front and back of the house. The drapes helped to protect against the cold, but only so much. He used pickled pine for the walls and ceiling of this, the most personal room in the house and Errol's favorite. In the southeast corner sat his leather-topped desk. In 1945 he will build an addition, placing a master bath near the den that included a black, marble-topped, deco-influenced sink, and a shower (right) that featured a glass outside wall frosted halfway up, offering a stunning view east, toward the Hollywood sign. (Photo by Mike Mazzone)

Above: Flynn's desk was modest and functional, and he placed lots of shelves within reach that held scripts, magazines, and his manuscript in progress, *Charlie Bow-tie*. In the winter, the sun raked across the sky and streamed in these windows during the day, as contrasted with sometimes chilly mountain nights in an age before energy-efficient windows.

Left: Of all the places at Mulholland Farm, the years were kindest to the den. After Flynn, Suzy Hamblen placed a desk here, as did Rick Nelson, who relished the passages in *My Wicked, Wicked Ways* in which Flynn described his affection for this room. (Photo by Mike Mazzone)

Above: Looking back from the fire-place, the view extended to the far wall of the living room, where Flynn had kept his radio/phonograph set, and where his Manet had hung. The bookshelves at right surrounded a glass-front ship-model display case backed with a map of San Diego Harbor, where he often moored the *Sirocco*. At the far end of the same wall, Flynn installed an in-wall speak-er. These can be found throughout the house, inside and out, filling the Farm with classical music. A pocket door, also in pickled pine, slid out from left to right to close the den off from the rest of the downstairs. Another pocket door slid out from left to right in the next archway, to close off the living room from the bar. (Photo by Mike Mazzone)

Right: Hardly grand, the den meas-ured only 18 x 19 feet. At left is the entrance cut for the 1945 addition. (Photo by Jack Marino)

Drapes open, drapes closed, drapes halfway; formal, with book and dog; informal with tea and no dog. Bert Six shot the den every which way. The black-and-white shots provide no perspective on Flynn's color scheme, with the burgundy leather chair, matching lamp shade, and stacked tables. He chose an equestrian theme, expressed in the fireplace andirons, fox-and-hound prints on the wall, and drapes showing wild horses running free, with the earthtones of the print complementing the surrounding wood grains. The chair was Flynn's favorite; he often slept here rather than in his bed.

The photo below, Flynn in dark shirt, was part of the whole-house shoot. The more formal Flynn-in-blazer shots were taken later, indicating that the studio sent Bert Six back to capture a yet-more introspective Flynn. Behind him in all poses are two of his favorite photos: at left, a shot taken by Peter Stackpole showing Flynn in the rigging of *Sirocco* during the *Life* Magazine photo shoot, and at right a portrait of FDR inscribed to Flynn. In the formal reshoot, little effort is made to declutter the low shelves behind him. The intention of the Doberman-and-blazer photos is clear: Errol Flynn isn't a bad boy, he's a cultured gentleman and scholar. (Note: The spot occupied by the FDR photo would become a doorway into the addition built in 1945.)

The original Warner Brothers caption for the photo at left reads: Errol Flynn, in a restful corner of his den, enjoys a cup of tea. Double-exposure windows are draped in hand-blocked linen, gaily colored in a hunting scheme. An autographed picture of the President can be seen on the built-in bookcase at the right. The chair in which he is sitting is of red moroccan leather, hand tooled. His latest picture for Warners is *Northern Pursuit*.

Left: The only known photograph of the interior of Errol Flynn's steam room with caricature art ordered up by the owner. On the wall at left, just out of frame, was a trap door leading to a narrow secret passageway that opened into a triangular viewing area into the ladies' room, with another trap door in the wall behind the bar. Flynn was probably sitting on the bench dead center in the photo late on the night of his White Mice Party when he was bombed and propositioned 20-year-old starlet Shirley Temple. She turned him down (she was with her husband!) and Flynn turned scornful. According to Temple: "'Goodbye, kid!'" he said, and waved me away with a sweeping gesture." (Photo by Jack Marino) Below left: Flynn ordered a three-car garage for his home. He liked fast, showy automobiles. It was here that Stuart Hamblen stuffed a mountain lion into the freezer and scared the milkman. (Photo by Mike Mazzone) Below: The western-most section of the house was rarely photographed because it was merely functional. It included a vestibule (just beyond the doorway at the foot of the stairs). Beyond it to the left was the small kitchen; to the right was the housekeeper's quarters, including a full bath. As shown in the photo on page 166, the Flynn, Hamblen, and Nelson families accessed the house most often via the doorway beside the garage. (Photo by Jack Marino)

Upon entering the house via the main poolside door, visitors saw the dining room to the right, which was still magnificent in the 1980s, and the spiral staircase ahead. Said Gunnar Nelson of his father's last road trip, "To this day I remember when our dad was getting ready to go on the road with his big green suitcases at the bottom of the stairs, waiting for the car to arrive to take him to the airport."[170]

(Photos by Jack Marino)

Left: The nautically inspired spiral staircase wound upward from a wide mouth at the bottom to a narrow passage up top. Arrival at the head of the stairs yielded a window dead ahead. Under it, in Flynn's day, stood a ship model in a glass case. Closets stood ahead at 10 and 2 o'clock. A hard left led into the aqua bedroom. Just to the right of the stairway was the yellow bedroom. Farther to the right, past a hallway of closet doors, stood Flynn's master bedroom. (Photo by Mike Mazzone)

Right: The yellow bedroom had the distinction of connecting to a full bath on one side (shared with the aqua bedroom) and a separate private powder room on the other. Kim Jaserie preferred to sleep in this bedroom to the aqua bedroom at the end of the house, which she found disquieting. When the Nelsons first moved in, this was Matthew's bedroom; Gunnar took the aqua bedroom. (Photo by Mike Mazzone)

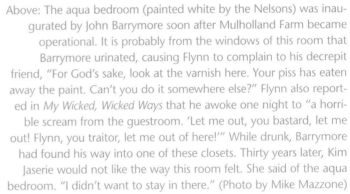

Above: The aqua bedroom (painted white by the Nelsons) was inaugurated by John Barrymore soon after Mulholland Farm became operational. It is probably from the windows of this room that Barrymore urinated, causing Flynn to complain to his decrepit friend, "For God's sake, look at the varnish here. Your piss has eaten away the paint. Can't you do it somewhere else?" Flynn also reported in *My Wicked, Wicked Ways* that he awoke one night to "a horrible scream from the guestroom. 'Let me out, you bastard, let me out! Flynn, you traitor, let me out of here!'" While drunk, Barrymore had found his way into one of these closets. Thirty years later, Kim Jaserie would not like the way this room felt. She said of the aqua bedroom. "I didn't want to stay in there." (Photo by Mike Mazzone)

Left: This was Tulley Brown's view out the door of the aqua bedroom as he watched what he decribed as a cloud of energy moving about in the hallway. In Flynn's day, a display case containing a ship model stood in the nook where light streams in. A brass plaque on the display case bore part of a poem written in 1916 by, ironically, a woman, Ella Wheeler Wilcox:

One ship drives east,
And another west,
By the self-same winds that blow,
'Tis the set of the sails
And not the gales,
That determines the way to go.

Flynn told Nora Eddington that these words conjured up adventure. "It's what keeps a man alive," he said. (Photo by Mike Mazzone)

Left: Doors and more doors. Visitors upstairs reported confusion about the many doors leading to rooms and closets. Rather than using a central hallway with rooms off of it, Flynn's narrow second-floor plan called for rooms leading directly to other rooms, with the exception of this small hallway with his clothes and shoe closets to the left. Beyond the second bulkhead is the master bedroom. The far doorway leads to Flynn's dressing room, with his master bath beyond that. (Photo by Mike Mazzone)

Right: The bedroom as it appeared in 1943 when photographed by Bert Six. Among its features were in-wall speakers above the bed and on the opposite wall. Said Nora Eddington of her first glimpse of it on a house tour by Flynn that same year, "The master bedroom was beautifully furnished, the wallpaper flowered, the rug bluish, the bedspread ruffled and the bed a kind of super king-size. It seemed almost unlived in, like a museum room where visitors are allowed to look but not enter."[171] In fact, Flynn often slept downstairs in his den. Two years later, thinking himself a phony, he would sit on this bed holding a pistol and contemplate suicide.

Right below: The same room in 1987. The Hamblens confirmed that Flynn had built a secret passageway to the first floor concealed behind the panel to the right of the fireplace. (Photo by Mike Mazzone)

Right: The 18 x 17-foot upstairs master bedroom was used by Flynn, Stuart and Suzy Hamblen, and by Kristen Nelson. It was last used by Matthew and Gunnar Nelson when they practiced their music, which would one day go multi-platinum. Said Gunnar: "It was our safe haven. We were able to put our instruments in the middle room with the fireplace, and we rehearsed forever. We spent like six years there developing our sound and it was nice to hitch a ride up to the house, and when Pop was in town visit with him, and get to work on what would later become the Nelson sound. If we didn't have that access, then there's no way we could have developed our music." (Photo by Jack Marino)

Flynn's large master bath featured a long countertop, walk-in shower, and heater unit to protect against the cold California nights. Up until 1945, the house ended at the doorway. When Flynn married Nora Eddington and their daughter Deirdre was born, he added on a nursery accessed only through the master bath. The Hamblens enlarged this room after a fire heavily damaged the nursery. Tracy Nelson used the bedroom and this bath until she moved out to attend college. (Photos by Mike Mazzone)

Located directly above Flynn's den, and with one wall composed of the chimney, baby Deirdre's nursery became an oddly shaped dorm room with a dog-leg right when expanded by the Hamblens. Here the grandkids played en masse and experienced lights switching on and off, which sent them scurrying to their "Nana and Pappy." Years later, Tracy Nelson said the blinds would roll up of their own accord, the toilet would flush, and the shower door would open and close. Gunnar Nelson said that he felt the weight of an unseen presence sit on the edge of his bed. Psychic Nancy Myer said she felt the overwhelming loneliness in this room of a woman whose love of Errol Flynn had gone unrequited. (Top photo by Jack Marino; bottom photo by Mike Mazzone)

Soon after the rape trial, in mid 1943, Warner Brothers Studio "still man" Bert Six was sent up to Mulholland Drive with a production team to photograph Errol Flynn at home. He captured the star in the hot summer sun, on the diving board of his pool (left), and before his rambling California Colonial. The pool was heated and nine feet deep. (John McElwee Collection)

Above: For many a guest, this was the first impression made by Mulholland Farm: garages and odd gables. The pool area was reached by turning left and walking around the housekeeper's bedroom (the structure in the left foreground) and then the dining wing. The balcony of the aqua bedroom is seen above the garage. The Flynns, Hamblens, and Nelsons all entered the house most often by climbing the stairs and entering through the kitchen door. (Photo by Robert Matzen) Below: The back side of the house as seen from the edge of the garage. (Photo by Mike Mazzone)

Right: This 1978 view shows the rambling nature of the house. The corner at left center with the small roof is Flynn's den. The exterior stairway leads to the attic. The gable beside the stairway is the attic space with the trap door above the two-way mirror. The ravine at left is the area that had been policed by Harve Presnell, yielding two truckloads of liquor bottles. (Photo by Jack Marino)

Below: Built in 1945, the nautically inspired stairs to the attic were in sad shape by the time they were photographed in June 1987. This stairway accessed the attic and also the trap door to the two-way mirror. The area of the wine cellar can be see through the stilts for the stairway. (Photo by Mike Mazzone)

Above: Exterior and interior view of the wine cellar, where Flynn also stored his 16mm film collection. The Hamblens stowed their black Labs here so the family could swim in the pool. As seen in the photo, the works from Errol Flynn's radio set (once in the living room) were relegated to the wine cellar by 1987. (Photos by Mike Mazzone)

Above: View from the porch toward the east; beyond the pool, two stone lions guard the gates to the tennis court stairway. (Photo by Mike Mazzone) Left: The brick stairway to the tennis court. (Photo by Mike Mazzone) Below: The tennis court as seen from the stairway landing. To the left is the patio viewing area. (Photo by Greg Maradei)

Right: This photo from the early 1960s shows the tennis court in relation to the barn (left) and casino (right) below. During an Easter egg hunt, children wait patiently for Stuart Hamblen to open the gate to the lower pasture. (Hamblen Family Collection) Below left and right: The lower pasture was important to all three families who owned Mulholland. Flynn rode his horses here and played with his kids. Egg hunts were held here for almost 20 years, and it was the center of the Hamblen grandchildren's play. Rick Nelson's sons, Gunnar and Matthew, enjoyed it as well. Matthew and I had a lot of room to forage and play army and all that stuff kids will do," says Gunnar Nelson. The lower pasture will be subdivided in the 1980s and become the site of luxury homes along Flynn Ranch Road. (Hamblen Family Collection)

Left: Parts of the lower pasture looked like Anywhere U.S.A. Said Bill Lindsay of this piece of ground, "It had pretty good-sized bushes and small trees—we found this little area where we could walk under the bushes and we made it a fort." Here Stuart Hamblen and three of his grandchildren go for a walk. Below: The closest known photo of Errol Flynn's casino, home of cockfights, poker tournaments, and debauchery that was never documented. In Stuart Hamblen's time the building was used for storage. Matthew and Gunnar Nelson would play in the vicinity. "I just remember playing around there," said Matthew, "and peeking in the windows and seeing it was empty and being afraid of it. I never even went inside it."[172] The photo below shows Stuart Hamblen and his oldest grandsons, Billy and Bobby Lindsay, quail hunting on the lower pasture. Bill said, "Pappy built a quail cage out of chicken wire with a tube and a trail of birdseed so they'd walk in through this tunnel. The quail could get in, but couldn't fly out. We had a pet quail, Jethro, from that adventure for *years*."[173] (Hamblen Family collection)

Above: This 1977 photo taken from Mulholland Drive shows the barn in full use by Stuart Hamblen. The casino seems to be in use as well, but isn't. The breadth of the lower pasture is visible, including the tree seen on page 169, used by the Hamblen grandchildren for play. (Photo by Jack Marino) Below: A few feet behind Flynn's property line rests James B. Lankershim under a 14-foot monument of stone and mortar. Lankershim was buried in 1931 overlooking the San Fernando Valley that he helped to develop. (The monument is visible in the photo above, at left center.) Flynn never commented on having a grave and its tall marker right next door. (Photo by Robert Matzen)

End Notes

1. Errol Flynn. Letter to Earl Conrad from Port Antonio, Jamaica, May 24, 1959.

2. Earl Conrad. *Errol Flynn: a Memoir.*

3. Florabel Muir. "The Fabulous Flynn," *Motion Picture,* April 1949.

4. Hobart High School records, September 1925.

5. John Hammond Moore. *The Young Errol: Flynn Before Hollywood.*

6. Basil Rathbone. *In and Out of Character.*

7. Dan Camp. "What's Biting Errol Flynn?" *Motion Picture,* December 1938.

8. Robert Matzen. Steven Hayes interview. March 29, 2008.

9. Dickson Morley. "A Real Day with Errol Flynn." *Screenland,* April 1939.

10. Nora Eddington Flynn Haymes as told to Cy Rice. *Errol and Me.*

11. Moore. *The Young Errol.*

12. Errol Flynn. New Guinea diary, January 13, 1933.

13. Letter from Errol Flynn to Hermann Erben, July 5, 1933.

14. Gerry Connelly. *Errol Flynn in Northampton.*

15. U.S. Department of Justice; Immigration and Naturalization Service. Permit No. N.I. 3276.

16. Academy of Achievement. Olivia de Havilland interview, Washington, D.C., October 5, 2006.

17. Buster Wiles with William Donati. *My Days with Errol Flynn: The Autobiography of a Stuntman.*

18. Rory Flynn. *The Baron of Mulholland.*

19. William Best files. Errol Flynn papers. May 24, 1936.

20. William Best files. Errol Flynn papers. February 20, 1937.

21. Errol Flynn. *My Wicked, Wicked Ways.*

22. Dan Camp. "What's Biting Errol Flynn." *Motion Picture,* December 1939.

23. Morley. *Screenland.*

24. Tony Thomas, Rudy Behlmer, and Clifford McCarty. *The Films of Errol Flynn.*

25. Adela Rogers St. John. "Errol Flynn Begins Again." *Photoplay,* October 1943.

26. Josef Fegerl, editor. *Errol Flynn-Dr. Hermann F. Erben: A Friendship of Two Adventurers, 1933-1940.*

27. Flynn. *My Wicked, Wicked Ways.*

28. Virginia Wood. "Errol Flynn Finally Talks!" *Screenland,* December 1944.

29. Academy of Achievement. Olivia de Havilland.

30. Wiles with Donati. *My Days with Errol Flynn.*

31. Hasking and Sells, CPAs. Errol Flynn equities in real and personal property. September 9, 1941.

32. Wood. *Screenland.*

33. Wood. *Screenland.*

34. Robert Matzen and Mike Mazzone. Hamblen Family interview. February 16, 2008.

35. Moore. *The Young Errol.*

36. Wiles with Donati. *My Days with Errol Flynn.*

37. Morley. *Screenland.*

38. Eddington Flynn Haymes. *Errol and Me.*

39. *Portrait of a Swashbuckler* [documentary]. A Mark Massari Production, 1983.

40. Ron Wood with Bill German. *Ron Wood.*

41. Robert Matzen. Gunnar Nelson interview. May 19, 2008.

42. R.J. Obringer memo. August 20, 1941. Warner Brothers Archives.

43. Flynn. *My Wicked, Wicked Ways.*

44. Raoul Walsh. *Each Man in His Time.*

45. Flynn. *My Wicked, Wicked Ways.*

46. Walsh. *Each Man in His Time.*

47. Robert Matzen. Harve Presnell interview. August 10, 2008.

48. Warner Brothers Archives, February 1942.

49. DSS Form 42A for Errol T. Flynn. Affidavit to Support Claim for Occupational Deferrment. February 5, 1942. Errol Flynn Legal File, Warner Brothers Archives.

50. Wiles with Donati. *My Days with Errol Flynn.*

51. T.C. Wright. Memo to R.J. Obringer. March 17, 1942. Warner Brothers Archives.

52. Flynn. *My Wicked, Wicked Ways.*

53. Viveca Lindfors. *Viveka…Viveca.*

54. Maureen O'Hara with John Nicoletti. *'Tis Herself.*

55. Rathbone. *In and Out of Character.*

56. Greer Garson. Introduction to *The Films of Errol Flynn.*

57. John Arnett. "Errol Flynn's Last Interview." New York *Post,* October 15, 1959.

58. Kirk Douglas. *The Ragman's Son.*

59. Flynn, *My Wicked, Wicked Ways.*

60. Flynn. *My Wicked, Wicked Ways.*

61. Jerry Giesler as told to Pete Martin. *The Jerry Giesler Story.*

62. Giesler. *The Jerry Giesler Story.*

63. Giesler. *The Jerry Giesler Story.*

64. Florabel Muir. *Headline Happy.*

65. Muir. *Headline Happy.*

66. Linda Christian. *Linda: My Own Story.*

67. Wiles with Donati. *My Days with Errol Flynn.*

68. Giesler. *The Jerry Giesler Story.*

69. Muir. *Headline Happy.*

70. Giesler. *The Jerry Giesler Story.*

71. Christian. *Linda: My Own Story.*

72. United Press. "Mistrial Is Demanded in Flynn Case." January 16, 1943.

73. Giesler. *The Jerry Giesler Story.*

74. Wiles with Donati. *My Days with Errol Flynn.*

75. Robert Matzen. Joan Leslie interview. February 16, 2008.

76. Wiles with Donati. *My Days with Errol Flynn.*

77. Muir. *Headline Happy.*

78. Flynn. *My Wicked, Wicked Ways.*

79. Wiles with Donati. *My Days with Errol Flynn.*

80. Rudy Behlmer, editor. *Inside Warner Brothers (1935-1951).*

81. Jack Warner. *My First Hundred Years in Hollywood.*

82. Bert Six started out at Warner Brothers in the 1930s as a portrait and keybook-still photographer. By 1940 he had earned a favorable reputation among the top Warners stars, including Flynn, and shot for top productions, including *The Dawn Patrol* and *The Private Lives of Elizabeth and Essex.* By 1943 Six was the perfect choice for a project as important as salvaging Errol Flynn's reputation. In 1945 he became the head of the Warner Brothers still photography department, where he remained until Jack Warner failed to renew the contract of "Bert Six, stillman," in 1949.

83. Flynn. *My Wicked, Wicked Ways.*

84. Walter Logan. "Mountbatten's HQ Plushest of the War." The Pittsburgh *Press.* September 2, 1979.

85. Warner Brothers Archives.

86. Lawrence Grobel. *The Hustons.*

87. John Huston. *An Open Book.*

88. Associated Press. "Actor Flynn Down for Short Count in 'One-Punch' Fight." April 10, 1945.

89. Lyn Tornabene. *Long Live the King.*

90. Marion Cooper. "Flynn Versus Flynn." *Photoplay,* June 1946.

91. James R. Silke. *Here's Looking at You, Kid.*

92. Flynn. *My Wicked, Wicked Ways.*

93. *Screenland.* April 1939.

94. Flynn. *My Wicked, Wicked Ways.*

95. "Flynn's First Fling." *Time,* February, 25, 1946.

96. Flynn. *My Wicked, Wicked Ways.*

97. Robert Stack with Mark Evans. *Straight Shooting.*

98. Louella O. Parsons. "Errol Flynn's Wife to Seek Early Divorce." Los Angeles *Examiner,* February 9, 1949.

99. Matzen. Steven Hayes interview.

100. Pat O'Brien. *The Wind at My Back.*

101. Ben Hecht. *Esquire,* December 1945.

102. Flynn. *My Wicked, Wicked Ways.*

103. John McElwee's Greenbriar Picture Shows web site (www.greenbriarpictureshows.blogspot.com), launched in 2005, is "dedicated to the great days of movie exhibition."

104. Warner Brothers Archives.

105. David Gelman. "Errol Flynn: His Life and Loves Part II." New York *Post,* October 18, 1959.

106. Telegram from Jack Warner to Errol Flynn. June 5, 1947. Warner Brothers Archives.

107. Stephen Longstreet. "Errol Flynn: Gentlemanly Rogue." *Close Ups: The Movie Star Book.*

108. Jean Negulsesco. Warner Brothers memo. May 6, 1947. Warner Brothers Archives.

109. *The Adventures of Errol Flynn* [documentary].

110. Lindfors. *Viveka…Viveca.*

111. O'Hara. *'Tis Herself.*

112. Hedy Lamarr. *Ecstasy and Me.*

113. Hank Kaufman. "Is There a New Errol?" *Silver Screen,* May 1954.

114. Patrice Wymore. "My Life with Errol Flynn." *Silver Screen,* July 1951.

115. Errol Flynn to Al Blum from Mulholland Farm, February 7, 1952.

116. Flynn. *The Baron of Mulholland.*

117. Flynn. *The Baron of Mulholland.*

118. Errol Flynn to Justin Golenbock, October 2, 1955.

119. Los Angeles *Examiner,* October 10, 1955.

120. Errol Flynn to Justin Golenbock, October 30, 1955.

121. Art Buchwald. "Gentlemen Never Tell." New York *Herald-Tribune,* July 6, 1958.

122. Coroner's Report of Inquiry as to the Cause of Death of Flynn, Errol Leslie. October 15, 1959.

123. Louella O. Parsons. "Errol was Replica of Roles He Played." New York *Journal-American,* October 17, 1959.

124. Bill Slocum. "Errol Was Sharp as a Whip with a Quip." New York *Mirror,* October 18, 1959.

125. Flynn. *The Baron of Mulholland.*

126. Sarah Hamilton. "The Mickey Flynn." *Photoplay,* August 1948.

127. Matzen. Steven Hayes interview.

128. Harry Crocker. "Behind the Makeup." Los Angeles *Examiner,* February 15, 1949.

129. Shirley Temple Black. *Child Star.*

130. Billy Graham. *Just As I Am.*

131. Turner. *The Adventures of Errol Flynn.*

132. Suzy Hamblen. *Serendipities: Mulholland Farm.*

133. Matzen. Harve Presnell interview.

134. Robert Matzen. Bill Lindsay interview. August 17, 2008.

135. Robert Matzen. Tulley Brown interview. August 10, 2008.

136. Matzen and Mazzone. Hamblen family interview.

137. Mike Mazzone. Judy Whisenant interview. October 24, 2008.

138. Laurie Jacobson and Mark Wanamaker. *Hollywood Haunted.*

139. Regan McMahon. "Rick Nelson: Back to Schooldays." *Bam,* January 16, 1981.

140. Leda Carmody reminiscence.

141. Robert Matzen. Regan McMahon interview. March 17, 2008.

142. McMahon. *Bam.*

143. Philip Bashe. *Teenage Idol, Travelin' Man: The Complete Biography of Rick Nelson.*

144. Bashe. *Teenage Idol, Travelin' Man.*

145. Robert Matzen. Robert Florczak interview. June 10, 2008.

146. Joel Selvin. *Ricky Nelson: Idol for a Generation.*

147. Selvin. *Ricky Nelson: Idol for a Generation.*

148. Matzen. Regan McMahon interview.

149. National Transportation Safety Board Identification: DCA86AA012.

150. Matzen. Gunnar Nelson interview.

151. Robert Matzen. Matthew Nelson interview. May 21, 2008.

152. Lamarr. *Ecstasy and Me.*

153. Peter Haining. *The Last Gentleman.*

154. Robert Matzen. Nancy Myer interview. July 20, 2008.

155. Matzen. Harve Presnell interview.

156. Matzen and Mazzone. Hamblen family interview.

157. Matzen and Mazzone. Hamblen family interview.

158. Matzen. Matthew Nelson interview.

159. Matzen. Tulley Brown interview.

160. Matzen. Gunnar Nelson interview.

161. Jacobson and Wanamaker. *Hollywood Haunted.*

162. Matzen and Mazzone. Hamblen family interview.

163. Robert Matzen and Mike Mazzone. Jack Marino interview. February 15, 2008.

164. Matzen and Mazzone. Hamblen family interview.

165. Matzen. Matthew Nelson interview.

166. Eddington Flynn Haymes. *Errol and Me.*

167. Christian. *Linda: My Own Story.*

168. Lake with Bain. *Veronica.*

169. Flynn. *My Wicked, Wicked Ways.*

170. Matzen. Gunnar Nelson interview.

171. Eddington Flynn Haymes. *Errol and Me.*

172. Matzen. Matthew Nelson interview.

173. Matzen. Bill Lindsay interview.

Book-Length Sources

Bashe, Philip. *Teenage Idol, Travelin' Man*. New York: Hyperion, 1992.

Behlmer, Rudy, Editor. *Inside Warner Bros. (1935-1951)*. New York: Viking Penguin, Inc., 1985.

Black, Shirley Temple. *Child Star*. New York: McGraw Hill, 1988.

Christian, Linda. *Linda: My Own Story*. New York: Dell Publishing Co., Inc., 1962.

Connelly, Gerry. *Errol Flynn in Northampton.* Northrants: Domra Publications, 1994.

Conrad, Earl. *Errol Flynn: A Memoir*. New York: Dodd, Mead, & Company, 1978.

De Havilland, Olivia. *Every Frenchman Has One*. New York: Random House, 1962.

Douglas, Kirk. *The Ragman's Son*. New York: Simon & Schuster, 1988.

Fegerl, Josef. *Errol Flynn Dr. Hermann F. Erben: A Friendship of Two Adventurers 1933-1940*. Vienna: Peter Pospischil, 1985.

Flynn, Errol. *Beam Ends*. New York: Longmans Green and Co., 1937.

Flynn, Errol. *My Wicked, Wicked Ways*. New York: G.P. Putnam's Sons, 1959.

Flynn, Errol. *Showdown*. New York: Sheridan House, 1946.

Flynn, Rory. *The Baron of Mulholland: A Daughter Remembers Errol Flynn*. 2007.

Frady, Marshall. *Billy Graham: A Parable of American Righteousness*. Boston: Little, Brown and Company, 1979.

Giesler, Jerry as told to Pete Martin. *The Jerry Giesler Story*. New York: Simon and Schuster, 1960.

Goodman, Ezra. *The Fifty-five Year Decline and Fall of Hollywood*. New York: Simon & Schuster, 1961.

Graham, Billy. *Just As I Am: The Autobiography of Billy Graham*. San Francisco: Zondervan, 1997.

Grobel, Lawrence. *The Hustons*. New York: Charles Scribners' Sons, 1989.

Haining, Peter. *The Last Gentleman: A Tribute to David Niven*. London: W.H. Allen, 1984.

Haymes, Nora Eddington Flynn as told to Cy Rice. *Errol and Me*. New York: Signet Books, 1960.

Henreid, Paul. *Ladies Man: An Autobiography*. New York: St. Martin's Press, 1984.

Huston, John. *An Open Book*. New York: Alfred A. Knopf, 1981.

Jacobson, Laurie and Wanamaker, Marc. *Hollywood Haunted: A Ghostly Tour of Filmland*. Santa Monica: Angel City Press, 1994.

Keyes, Evelyn. *Scarlett O'Hara's Younger Sister*. Secaucus: Lyle Stuart Inc., 1977.

Lake, Veronica with Donald Bain. *Veronica: The Autobiography of Veronica Lake*. Secaucus: The Citadel Press, 1971.

Lamarr, Hedy. *Ecstasy and Me: My Life as a Woman.* Bartholomew House, 1966.

Marble, Alice. *Courting Danger: My Adventures in World-Class Tennis, Golden-Age Hollywood, and High-Stakes Spying.* New York: St. Martin's Press, 1992.

McNulty, Thomas. *The Life and Career of Errol Flynn.* Jefferson, NC: McFarland and Co., Inc., 2004.

Lindfors, Viveca. *Viveka-Viveca.* New York: Everest House, 1981.

Moore, John Hammond. *The Young Errol: Flynn Before Hollywood.* Sydney: Angus and Robertson, Publishers, 1975.

Muir, Florabel. *Headline Happy.* New York: Henry Holt and Company, 1950.

O'Brien, Pat. *The Wind at My Back.* New York: Doubleday & Company, 1964.

O'Hara, Maureen with John Nicoletti. *'Tis Herself.* New York: Simon & Schuster, 2004.

Peary, Danny. *Close-Ups: Intimate Profiles of Movie Stars by Their Co-Stars, Directors, Screenwriters, and Friends.* New York: Workman Publishing Co., 1978.

Rathbone, Basil. *In and Out of Character.* New York: Doubleday & Company, 1962.

Selvin, Joel. *Ricky Nelson: Idol for a Generation.* Chicago: Contemporary Books, 1990.

Silke, James R. *Here's Looking at You, Kid: 50 Years of Fighting, Working and Dreaming at Warner Bros.* Boston: Little, Brown and Company, 1976.

Stack, Robert with Mark Evans. *Straight Shooting.* New York: Macmillan Publishing Co., Inc., 1980.

Thomas, Tony, Rudy Behlmer, and Clifford McCarty. *The Films of Errol Flynn.* Secaucus: The Citadel Press, 1969.

Thomas, Tony, Editor. *From a Life of Adventure: The Writings of Errol Flynn.* Secaucus: The Citadel Press, 1980.

Thomey, Tedd. *The Loves of Errol Flynn: The Tempestuous Life Story of One of Hollywood's Most Flamboyant Screen Stars.* Derby, CT: Monarch Books, Inc., 1962.

Tornabene, Lyn. *Long Live the King: A Biography of Clark Gable.* New York: G.P. Putnam's Sons, 1976.

Walsh, Raoul. *Each Man in His Time: The Life Story of a Director.* New York: Farrar, Straus and Giroux, 1974.

Warner, Jack L. with Dean Jennings. *My First Hundred Years in Hollywood: An Autobiography.* New York: Random House, 1964.

Wiles, Buster with William Donati. *My Days with Errol Flynn.* Santa Monica: Roundtable Publishing, 1989.

Wilkerson, Tichi and Marcia Borie. *The Hollywood Reporter: The Golden Years.* New York: Arlington House, Inc., 1984.

Wood, Ron with Bill German. *Ron Wood: The Works.* New York: Harper and Row, 1987.

Young, Perry Deane. *Two of the Missing: A Reminiscence of Some Friends in the War.* New York: Coward, McCann & Geoghegahn, Inc., 1975.

Index